How the News Makes Us Dumb

THE DEATH
OF WISDOM
IN AN
INFORMATION
SOCIETY

C. John Sommerville

InterVarsity Press
Downers Grove, Illinois

InterVarsity Press
P.O. Box 1400, Downers Grove, IL 60515
World Wide Web: www.ivpress.com
E-mail: mail@ivpress.com

*InterVarsity Press® is the book-publishing division of InterVarsity Christian Fellowship/USA®, a
student movement active on campus at hundreds of universities, colleges and schools of nursing in the
United States of America, and a member movement of the International Fellowship of Evangelical
Students. For information about local and regional activities, write Public Relations Dept.,
InterVarsity Christian Fellowship/USA, 6400 Schroeder Rd., P.O. Box 7895, Madison, WI 53707-7895,
or visit the IVCF website at <www.intervarsity.org>.*

Cover photograph: Greg Pease/Tony Stone Images

ISBN 0-8308-2203-8

Printed in the United States of America ♾

Library of Congress Cataloging-in-Publication Data

Sommerville, C. John (Charles John), 1938-
    How the news makes us dumb / C. John Sommerville.
        p.   cm.
    Includes bibliographical references.
    ISBN 0-8308-2201-1 (pbk. : alk. paper)
    *1. Journalism—United States—Objectivity. 2. Mass media—United
States—Objectivity. 3. Press and politics—United States.*
    I. Title.
    PN4888.025S66   1999
    302.23'0973—dc21   99-10870
                                                                                            CIP

P   21   20   19   18   17   16   15   14   13   12   11   10   9   8   7

Y   19   18   17   16   15   14   13   12   11   10   09   08   07   06

For Patti, Richard, Brad,
Bob, Rodney and the WWW

Preface

As in all books of media criticism, the examples used here are not absolutely up to date. Actually that will help demonstrate this book's thesis. Items in the news always seem a little homeless and disconnected when we stumble on them later. We have forgotten what they once meant, what the bigger picture was. That is because the news industry succeeded in destroying the context of those items, which is the best way to make money off them. Read on to find out what we're talking about.

1
Why
the News
Can't Be Fixed

Why on earth would we need another critique of the news when there have been so many recently?[1] Critics have come at the subject from every possible angle, one would think. Some concentrate on an alleged bias—the conservative bias of publishers or the liberal bias of editors. This book is not about that or about the techniques of manipulation. Others criticize the irresponsibility of journalists who are trying to attain celebrity status; that won't be our main point. There could be more books on the sheer incompetence of reporters, who cannot hope to become expert on all they try to cover. Other books have been about the oversimplification of TV news and still others about the corporate concentration of news in a few networks and chains. We won't get into any of that.

These are things to worry about, for sure. All the abuses that critics complain about have become more obvious recently. That is because accountants have learned better how to calculate the bottom line for publishers fixated on profits. But there is something that all of these critiques have missed and that goes deeper than any of them. It is that our news is daily.

It will take a short book to show all the ways that dailiness constitutes a bias all by itself. Of course, dailiness is necessary if we are to have a news industry. And that is why the news can't be fixed. Consuming this industry's "news product" actually makes us dumb.

In the last few years the tempo of news has increased, and now TV offers us hourly or even continuous reports. This adds to our problems. There is less time to check out reports, for instance. But that relates to sloppiness, which is not our theme. We want to concentrate on something deeper that is just as characteristic of our most respected newspapers as of our much-maligned networks. So I'll have just as much to say about our print media, to make sure I'm not misunderstood. TV only exaggerates the problems of periodicity.

All previous critiques of the media are full of blame and futile advice on how to fix the news. They are written by people who think news is important and who imagine that everyone reads it or at least watches it. They would be surprised at how many are giving it up and lie to pollsters about how much they read. Intellectuals—these critics and their audience—are unaware that they are leading a parade that has disbanded, for people have gone home to start building local communities to take the place of the pseudosociety constituted by our news.

This book will explain why we are losing interest in the news and why this is actually a *positive* sign. The American public may be showing a healthy suspicion not just of the kind of news we're getting but of the whole concept of daily news. So it would help to consider what news really is, as an industrial product, and how consuming too much of it has affected our minds.

This is the only critique of the media that welcomes its decline and that makes none of those futile recommendations for its improvement. News as we know it is developing in line with its essential nature. After three hundred years the news industry has reached its maturity and demonstrated its essential flaw. (I've traced part of this history in a more academic book.[2]) It is now apparent how it deconstructs our experience of the world and blocks the higher mental processes.

We cannot hope to break the news addiction of generations that were raised to mistake daily news for a part of nature. There are even philosophers, such as Jürgen Habermas, who think that the issue is not the periodical character of the news but rather who controls the media. They do not see how daily news cannot help being "colonized" by industry, with all that this means for the adulteration of its product. But if there are readers who are searching for an alternative to a debilitating news consciousness, this is the book.

If you are one of those people who doesn't like the news and doesn't exactly know why, this book should explain it. If you are one of those people who *likes* the news and thinks that it keeps you informed about the real world, you have an even greater need to read this book. But be warned that I won't be blaming the news, which is only fulfilling its essential nature. I am blaming those of us who still consume it. I am not arguing that the news is dumb but that we are.

We take the news industry and daily news production so much for granted that no one has tried to analyze the effects of dailiness. Unofficially, news just means things that you want to hear about and tell others about. News in that sense is a natural part of life. But what I am critiquing here is the product created by the news industry, which has a bad record of mental pollution. It is scary to realize that it is this news product that holds our society together, or pretends to do so, by creating a kind of virtual community.

The world hasn't always had a news industry. News used to come along irregularly, when something happened that was really important or interesting. To be honest, most days' news is neither. But the industry has to work on whatever they've got because they have to market their product daily.

And here we're getting to a main point. *The only reason for making news daily is to create an information industry.* You can't have a news *business* unless you pretend that the news is daily. If publishers waited for something important to happen, they might be idle for weeks and their capital assets would get rusty. So they have convinced us that every day is worthy of the same attention: "In the next thirty minutes your world will change; *Headline News* will be there to report it all."[3] Actually it didn't, and of course they couldn't. But "the world" of *Headline News* has become the world we live in, our virtual reality. Editors and broadcasters prod us along for the sake of their profits rather than for our enlightenment.

Defining News as a Product

By definition *the news* is what got into today's paper or broadcast. There were undoubtedly several hundred "events" yesterday with as great a claim to newsworthiness as the dozen that we heard about. After all, the real world is a big place—180-some countries, five or six billion people. The fact that the staff of CNN probably doesn't even know the names of a quarter of those countries doesn't mean that nothing important happens in them. But the events that didn't make today's papers will never be news. They might become part of the *history* of our time, being more important than most of our news in the long run. But news is what publishers think they can get us interested in and get us to pay for.

We can't even say that news events are more important than others. In fact, there is reason to doubt that. Important people don't like to be in the news. Power could probably be defined as the ability to keep oneself out of the news. Celebrities like to be in the news, and the media have found that we will pay as much to read about them as about important people. So we fill our minds with a lot of fun stories, while the powerful go about their business. For two weeks after Princess Diana died in that sad accident in 1997, one might have assumed that nothing else was happening in the world. We didn't hear about it if it did, since only a few events get to be news. We only have the patience for a few minutes of broadcast news or a few pages of a paper. Historians may eventually tell us that the world turned a corner at just that time. Maybe in some embassy or boardroom or laboratory or monk's cell some lever was pulled that set history on a new course. But it will never be news if it missed that first opportunity.

Really important information still circulates by word of mouth, not in the news media. Really important information circulates privately, among elites. That is what elites are—groups that control a certain kind of information. Important information is information that costs a lot, one way or another; what is left over gets into the newscast. The irony is that we imagine that news product is so much more.

I once saw a televised interview with actor Michael Douglas in which he was asked why he had such a reputation for erudition in the otherwise ditzy world of entertainment. His answer was that he read four newspapers each day. In other words, his mind is absolutely crammed with ephemera. The interviewer did not think to ask whether he had time to read anything in depth. Michael Douglas is not unintelligent; he just shares the dumbness of a society that has pretty much given up the serious investigation of any topic. We prefer the news treatment, which is careful not to tax our patience or our intelligence. But no number of newspapers will add up to real knowledge; the daily character of news treatment structures it to keep our minds small.

If you don't like my definition of news, take someone else's:

News is, first, what is interesting to the public and, second, what is new, always remembering that "newness is measured in newspaper offices in terms of minutes."[4] In the university where I work we were given "A Guide to Working with the Media," which reminds us that "reporters are usually under extremely tight deadlines, and a delay of a day, or even an hour, can mean the difference between favorable coverage and a lost opportunity or a reporter disinclined to turn to our university for help." I'm sure our philosophy department has never been any help to such an enterprise. Even if they were asked, they would be defeated by the fact that—as the guide warns—"Few 'sound bites' are more than 20 seconds long." It follows that universities are becoming more and more irrelevant to our "culture." None of the "big questions" will ever be news. Perhaps we should worry more about how we are spoiling our appetite with news and never getting around to the main course.

The product of the news business is *change*, not wisdom. You need to go elsewhere for wisdom. Wisdom has to do with seeing things in their largest context, whereas news is structured in a way that destroys the larger context. You have to do certain things to information if you want to sell it on a daily basis. You have to make each day's report seem important. And you do that by reducing the importance of its context. If readers were aware of the bigger story it would diminish today's contribution to that story. So news-industry profits absolutely depend on dumbing us down by deconstructing our world by dailiness. In reporting today's news they have to make us want to come back *tomorrow* for more news—more change. Tomorrow the implication will be that today's report can now be forgotten. The rest of this book will describe how this affects our thinking about politics, values, science, culture—everything. Bias and incompetence will have nothing to do with it, only dailiness.

I won't be proving all my points (whatever that would mean).

I'll only be reminding you of things you've seen in the news and asking you to consider their likely effect. We won't need statistics on news stories or on reader response to recognize some things we've all been ignoring.

There are no villains in this story. I am as disappointed about this as you are, but in a fundamental sense the industry can't help itself. Once you accept the idea of daily publication, a lot of other things follow. If there were villains, we could sentence them to several months of community service or send them back for refresher courses in the liberal arts. Ultimately, it is the consumers of news who are to blame; we have acquired an addiction, and newspeople are just supplying the market.

The News Goes into Free Fall

Several recent developments have caused even newspeople to sense that something is going wrong with their enterprise. For instance, they still complain about our first national newspaper, *USA Today*. When it appeared in 1982 with its big headlines and little stories, its charts and color bars, it was scorned as a vulgarization of the news, a trivialization of true journalism. But no one was surprised when it arrived. Everyone seemed to realize that it simply accelerated existing trends, which is what made it so scary. Newspeople were quick to realize that everyone would want to copy it. And they have.

What did *USA Today* show about the news? It gave us "reality" in simple terms, with a concentration on ourselves. By jumping from subject to subject it showed very clearly that news deals in the ephemeral—the flotsam and foam on the surface of history. It was pretty clear that it did not see its job as telling us what this all means in the bigger picture. Nobody has that job anymore.

If news were just one of many things that we read each day, it wouldn't have the same impact. If we would read science, the classics, history, theology or political theory at any length, we would make much better sense of today's events. But we don't. We're too busy to manage anything but the news, and we're getting almost too busy even for that. So the papers and the TV stations are learning to package it for us in ever more "attractive" forms.

My local newspaper, the *Gainesville Sun* (a *New York Times* subsidiary) has taken on the *USA Today* look. Less than 20 percent of the space on the front page is actually devoted to small print. The other 80 percent is given over to what might be termed "visual excitement": large headlines, color photos, directions on what you will find inside. Most of this visual excitement is crammed into the space that can be seen through the vending-machine windows to grab customers who are deciding which of the papers promises the most excitement. What does this excitement have to do with news? you ask. It *is* the news: change, variety, shock.

Of course there is more than excitement in newspapers. There is entertainment and edification in "Dear Abby" and *Doonesbury*. There is information of importance to *your* life, such as notices of gatherings and sales and events that you won't want to miss. There are sports reports and health tips. Not everything in a newspaper is news. But this other stuff would not justify a *daily* edition. The way you are induced to buy the industry's product every day is by being offered the excitement and the change that constitutes the news of the day.

I'm not going to argue that we were better off when the whole front page was small print and long gray columns. The effect of that news was the same. All I am saying is that the industry's desperation to sell today's and tomorrow's news is beginning to make us more aware of what has always been wrong with news—its desire to please and flatter and excite us so that we will come back for tomorrow's issue.

You might ask, "Well what do you expect? Of course the media have got to make their product attractive. They have to make a living." If you don't like the word *greed,* you could say they have "a responsibility to their stockholders." Just so. Once the stock of news corporations is sold publicly, Wall Street insists on the same profit level from them as from any detergent company or fashion house. We should be under no illusions about the fact that the point of news is profit and not, say, "truth." If the goal were enlightenment, there would be days when the paper would have to be several times bigger and others in which publishers wouldn't bother printing one.

If one admits that the media are mainly in the business of selling something, of getting people interested, then one begins to erase the line separating the *New York Times* and the *National Enquirer.* In fact, we are frequently reminded that where the tabloids lead, the "respectable press" will soon—actually must—follow. "You get sucked in," Leslie Stahl admits. "Everybody knows how hard the *Washington Post* worked not to print the Paula Jones story. There does come a point when a story is so 'out there' that a news organization is foolish if it doesn't."[5] News is what it is. What we need to be reminded of is that things of first importance cannot be made into news.

It's nice that philosophy is not organized in corporations that need to show a competitive profit margin. Philosophy would certainly become more lively if it had to be produced and marketed daily, but something else would be lost. Fortunately, our philosophers are still as pure as hermits. And just as lonely.

Media critics like to worry over the *National Enquirer,* and they shame other papers by making comparisons. We treat it as if it were a caricature of real news. Actually, the *Enquirer* shows the ripening of the news and where the industry is headed. Remember our definition: news is what sells newspapers. In the old days some editors took a high-handed approach and tried to give the public what they thought grown-up, serious-minded people should know. But the dynamics of the enterprise have defeated them. Newspeople have gotten smarter about the business they're in, and we've gotten dumber. They know that deep down we don't care if our daily news is entirely authentic as long as it is entertaining, like professional wrestling. So we can expect to see even the most respectable newspapers gradually becoming more and more like the *National Enquirer.* And if you doubt that statement, take a look at a newspaper from fifty years ago to see how far we've come already.

There also is much worry about how sketchy TV news is in comparison with the more respected papers. But the same dynamics are involved, as we will see. The commercial possibilities involved in both enterprises depend on the commodification of their product, chopping information into periodical reports that we can be forced to pay for, one way or another.

Despite increasingly frantic efforts to keep us entertained, there is evidence of several kinds of decline in the news business, especially among the rising generation. The news itself sometimes reports figures on a decline of consumption for newspapers, newsmagazines and newscasts. And if the decline in sales and viewership were not troubling enough, newspeople also find that their credibility is declining "significantly" among the public.[6] And beyond that, we are showing ourselves to be less "informed" as a result of media efforts. Editors are bewildered by what they have done to us. The *New Yorker* complained on April 15, 1985, that by that time "young people" knew almost nothing about the Vietnam War, which had absolutely filled the news for ten years when the writer of the article was growing up. He reported on an army recruit who did not know that the United States had lost that war. By contrast, as he observed, the Poles, who had not trusted their press for many years, could remember their whole history despite government efforts to suppress it.

Is News a Business or a Profession?

When newspeople begin their soul-searching about these trends, they start to wonder whether they even have a soul. On March 5, 1990, Carl Bernstein (of Watergate fame) wrote an agonized essay in *Time* that lamented how celebrity millionaire Donald Trump and his wife had crowded statesman Nelson Mandela off the front page. Bernstein kept referring to "real news," "the truth," "real journalism" and "appearance as opposed to substance," implying that there was a time when journalists could actually decide—from among the thousands of things that happen each day around the world—which half-dozen were most "important."

This is a fantasy. The thinking of industry bosses, from the seventeenth century until now, is revealed in the speeches reported from an April 1989 meeting of publishers. Those speeches pointed up the need to appeal to a generation that has almost given up reading. Market analysts had told them that a new generation's buying habits depended more on packaging than on content. The solution seemed to be a mix of "traditional news" with useful information such as lists of daycare centers and instructions on where to register to vote. It doesn't take a prophet to foresee that the trend will be not toward Bernstein's effort at greater seriousness but toward an even more frantic glitziness.

("But," you ask, "what about Bernstein and Watergate? Didn't his reporting do a world of good?" I would be the last to deny it. The question is whether that sort of crusade was best done in daily newspapers. Might daily reporting actually have been a poor way to conduct such an investigation, except in terms of profits? The muckraking journalists who made such an impact in the Progressive Era published their reports in magazines and books, not in newspapers. We'll come back to this question.)

We will not join the mourners for the noble ideal of real news. In the history to which I referred, one will find that as soon as newspapers started in Europe, around 1620, the primary concern was not the search for truth but rather excitement and profits. And the complaints with which we are familiar began within five years of the origins of the periodical press. There was a difference between then and now, to be sure, but the difference was in the audience. In those days news was a very small bit of what people took in, being balanced by a rich culture, books and conversation. We are now seeing what happens when one depends entirely on daily reports, with their decontextualizing and deconstructing tendencies.

If you insist on news, there is only one kind: an addictive substance that you never get enough of. And we have become jaded, requiring an ever-increasing level of excitement. It had better be good or our minds may wander. The industry, like any good entrepreneur, does its best to give us what we want, and what we want is a limited number of stories that we can follow for a few days and that involve us in some way. What we get is a teeny bit of our world, vastly enlarged to fill our vision.

"From CNN—this is the world today." What do you think would follow such an imposing introduction? Lengthy reports on those 180-some countries and their countless inhabitants, the joys and miseries and humdrum of real life in all its boring variety? Hardly. Who wants to hear about the whole world today? We only want a little excitement. So depending on the network, we get nine to thirteen stories in a half-hour span, stories that can seem pretty sensational if you give them a particular slant. This news has a magical quality: if you have a compartment in your brain that is set aside for the news, it will always be full. Even if there were only one story per day, that story, however trivial it might seem later, would absolutely fill your screen. Just one story can overspread the whole front page, seeming all-important—that day. For news has no sense of scale. It concentrates the mind when we thought it was to broaden the mind.

Why Intellectuals Are Clueless

The greatest irony in our story is the fact that our intellectuals are less likely to have turned against the news culture than others. While they might scorn the low-calorie product that the networks provide, they often lament the ignorance of those who aren't following the reports in the prestige press. Of course, if the masses were to give up on news altogether, this elite would not be able to demonstrate its superiority, which is gained from feeding higher on the news chain. But it is surprising to see them more concerned about identifying with the news-fact discourse than with the cultural heritage in which many of them were trained.

Our universities do not fight the narrowed vision that is part of the news concept. I used to be incredulous when I saw universities schedule TV newsreaders as campus speakers. Why would anyone be interested in what they had to say when no one was handing them a script? I am wiser now. I now realize that newspeople really do make the news. They create it—a reality that we depend on, a miniature world that we look in on every day to assure ourselves that everything is under control or at least that we know the worst. These people, or their handlers, decide on a few developments that they hope we will be interested in and choose the tone and the slant that will grab us. Then they poll us to see whether they're succeeding.

News may have little to do with a search for truth, but it does reveal our "popular culture." And that is the new substitute for philosophy, even in colleges. Some elite institutions (Harvard, for instance) ask their applicants which newspapers or newsmagazines they read regularly. Others (Davidson, for example) make their accepted freshmen read some newspaper—usually the *New York Times* or *Washington Post*—during the summer before they arrive at school. This is so they will be "informed" and so the student body will be more challenging and vibrant.

Actually, reading these papers will create confused and scatterbrained students. Think I'm kidding? Consider the following headlines:

• *Washington Post*, September 11, 1988: "Zia Death Probe Said to Indicate Sabotage"
• *New York Times*, same day: "No Sabotage Clues Seen in Zia Crash"
• *Washington Post*, October 16, 1988: "Iran Offers to Accept Iraqi Kurds"
• *New York Times*, same day: "Iran Is Said to Close Its Border to Iraqi Kurds"

• *Washington Post*, October 25, 1988: "Prosperity Eludes Grenada 5 Years After Invasion"
• *New York Times*, same day: "5 Years Later, Grenada Is Tranquil and Thriving"

• *Washington Post*, October 26, 1988: "Washington Post Profit Up 23 Percent in Third Quarter"
• *New York Times*, same day: "Profits Fall at Washington Post"

I'm not making this up. These quotes were collected by the readers of the *New Republic* over the course of a few months. But wait, things get worse.

• *Washington Post*, December 23, 1988: "Drexel Settlement Is Taken in Stride by Wall Street"
• Same paper, same day: "Drexel Case Likely to Have Serious Impact on Wall Street"

• *New York Times*, March 24, 1989: "In Autos, U.S. Makes Strides"
• Same paper, same day: "U.S. Vehicle Sales Are Sluggish"

What if you relied on one of these papers as your window on the world? What if you relied on both of them? What if sometimes you just skimmed headlines without getting into the fine print? And what makes you think that either one of these papers got it right?

Did you notice, by the way, that the examples given above were taken from a period of just a few months? Think how confused Michael Douglas must have been. And the problem was not only with those two papers.

• *San Francisco Examiner,* **November 13, 1988: "Wright Takes Hard Line with Bush"**

• *Sacramento Bee,* **same day: "Wright Holds Olive Branch for Bush"**

• *Times* **(London), December 17, 1988: "American Jewish Reaction—Outrage at Policy Change"**

• *Guardian* **(London), same day: "Lack of Jewish Political Outcry Causes Surprise in Washington"**

• *Los Angeles Times,* **November 1, 1988: "Fed Intervenes to Provide a Lift for Sagging Dollar"**

• **Same paper, same day: "Bond Prices Get Big Lift from Stronger Dollar"**

• *Chicago Tribune,* **December 7, 1988: "Gorby Fever Sweeps Manhattan"**

• **Same paper, same day: "New Yorkers Take Soviet Visit in Stride"**

You might think that we have only demonstrated that headline writers get sloppy and don't always read enough of the story. No doubt that can happen. But that is not the most likely explanation for the high number and regularity of these contradictions. There is a more disturbing possibility.

Newswriters can't know which way things are moving. The dynamics of periodical publication create a world that is lacking a time dimension. But reporters have to make a guess as to the future importance of present events, or else those events cannot be assigned any importance. Readers want to know how today's events fit into a bigger picture; they want prophets to lead them. Unfortunately, the bigger picture is exactly what news destroys in hyping today's report. So to suggest the historical significance of today's event, newspeople put some kind of "spin" on the story that amounts to their guess about future developments. To give the story any kind of conclusiveness they must decide which *part* of a story to emphasize, and hence these different headlines—not just different but directly contradictory.

In 1730 the Grub Street Journal, *a London periodical, was started for the very purpose of printing conflicting reports from rival papers side by side in its pages. It became popular. Oddly enough, people kept right on buying papers. Will we make the same mistake? Even when we catch the papers in distortion—just about any time they report something of which we have personal knowledge—we still come back to them for more. We know it is insubstantial fare, like enchanted food, but we need that daily fix. Why can't we "just say no"?*

Perhaps we could if we delved a little deeper into how the news operates.

2

News Product as Creative Expression

- - - - - - - - - - -

A lot has been written lately about how competitive the news business is becoming. A new breed of CEO is closing down one newspaper after another in order to raise the profit margins of our "consciousness industry" conglomerates. For example, in 1995 Mark Willes, chairman of Times Mirror, declared that his overriding goal was to "grow our earnings per share by fifty percent in 1996."[1] Imagine being an editor in this corporate world and having to worry about whether your paper or your program is on the chopping block. Imagine having to produce every day a new edition or a new broadcast that will sell itself, sell tomorrow's edition and beat out your increasingly energetic competitors. What do you do?

You would do what we intend to do—recall the techniques we have all seen used to grab our attention and sell the product. What is the formula for creating news product? How does the industry get us to come back for more?

The best way of getting customers to come back for tomorrow's edition is to offer "news as striptease." The last thing the newspeople want to do is end a good story. They want to string out any investigation as long as possible. In the Watergate era editors didn't have to worry about how to fill the front page for a matter of many months. The politicians were the only ones who seemed to want to "get all this behind us as soon as possible." And now that editors have decided that sex is as newsworthy as politics, we are constantly in the midst of some such striptease.

The economics of periodical publication require that newspeople not get to the bottom of things too soon. The longer it takes, the more news gets sold. So the investigation itself becomes their main interest, not the larger picture or the truth about the matter. The investigation is news, but the result of the investigation is something else—history, perhaps. Watergate is the classic example of this. Day by day enough bits of detail dribbled out to keep us coming back. Meanwhile, almost nothing else went on in the world, to judge from the papers. The solution to the Watergate puzzle didn't appear in the paper but in books, which few people read. And for years afterward reporters picked at loose threads in hopes that something would come undone and we could have another go at it.

Who is responsible for our periodic feeding frenzies? We are, of course. If we wanted the truth, we would wait for those books. But when newspeople wave the veils like Salome, our interest perks up. Their trick, of course, is to pretend they too are still surprised at the daily revelations. It reminds one of the Bedouin shepherds in Palestine who find ancient documents and tear them into little bits that they sell to archaeologists whenever they need some pocket money. This makes the scholars work a lot harder than they need to, but it's good economics. If we got our news at monthly intervals, we could save ourselves a lot of time. We would not have filled our minds with false leads and speculation. The question is whether we would have died of boredom in the meantime.

But What About Watergate?

Of course you are wondering, "Well who would have discovered Watergate if it hadn't been for those newspeople? Who would have tracked those leads into the White House itself? Don't we owe them a very great deal, and doesn't this justify a few excesses and some silliness?" Let's think about that. How did the *Washington Post* first learn of the Watergate break-in? A court in Washington had begun prosecuting the case. The subsequent investigation was handled by lawyers and detectives for the Democratic Party, the FBI, the federal judiciary and congressional committees, as well as by reporters. The reporters often got in the way of the investigation, as sources clammed up rather than have their stories misused in the media.

Don't get me wrong. I expect that the news made an important contribution during Watergate. But all that this proves is that we might want to buy a newspaper when there is an important story— every twenty years or so. More and more people are treating the news this way, as if they don't need newspapers in the meantime. Why would we need to subscribe during all the years in which what is developing can't be truly reported in daily bits? There will always be news junkies to keep the media going. Meanwhile the rest of us already seem to be learning to ignore the media the same way some people ignore the clergy these days, until they have something to solemnize in their otherwise drab lives.

If we only picked up a newspaper once a month, we would often conclude that nothing much had happened in the meantime, which may be the case. And yet those who have read every intervening issue are convinced that they live amidst dizzying change. In a way they do; at least their minds are kept in a whirl and their culture is churned. But the bureaucratic and commercial forces that run their lives, including the news business, remain unmoved. The business of the news is to create the illusion of change, which we seem to crave.

News as an Addiction

The techniques of stringing us along show that the news industry is not as interested in satisfying a hunger as in creating an addiction. News schedules create an emptiness that is to be filled by tomorrow's broadcast and the one after that. Truth, in any more final sense, is an anticlimax. Once all the veils have dropped, Truth runs off the stage, for the concealment is more exciting than whatever is underneath—if excitement is our goal.

There had better be something for the news to switch to when each of these investigations is over. Maybe it could be another serial rapist or hostage crisis. Those can keep us worried for two or three weeks. The terrorists hope it will so they can dramatize their issue, and newspeople are eager to oblige. The industry is not quick to admit when such a crisis is over. We will have continuing stories about the grieving widows, the suspected masterminds, airport security and what the government is doing about it all.

Government often does come to the aid of the news, given its fallibility and our unreasonable expectations. You may remember the U.S. invasion of Panama in December 1989. One of the first things the newspeople told us (the very first day) was that the government had probably miscalculated and gotten us into a long-term conflict. It seemed a reasonable proposition and is the kind of mistake that the news looks forward to. They envisioned American troops chasing after guerrillas for months, maybe years, while reporters reported possible sightings of the maddeningly elusive Manuel Noriega. Mounting casualty figures would be a standing rebuke to our overbearing leaders.

They had some tough luck there. The resistance collapsed, the American casualty count got stuck in the 20s, Noriega sneaked into the Vatican embassy and gave himself up. At the very least, newspeople hoped that they could sustain interest through a long trial, which might even force an investigation—a long, slow investigation—into President Bush's previous activities as CIA director. Otherwise they would have nothing to show for this military adventure. But that didn't happen either. So the Panama incursion will be history, to be sure, but it did not work out as news.

Celebrating Celebrities

There are other techniques for creating news when the government stays out of trouble. We can follow certain personalities who are identified as newsworthy. The industry has a file of people who are always news, to whom they can switch when things are slow. They are valued for their proneness to accident. The list changes. When I started putting these thoughts together the list included Shirley MacLaine, Colonel Muammar al-Qaddafi, Donald Trump, Madonna, Michael Jackson, Michael Jordan and Ted Kennedy. Returning to them gives us a sense of familiarity within the world's change. It makes the world our neighborhood, if that is not too childish a fantasy. Years later we find out what was really going on while we were stargazing. Later histories can tell us, if we're still reading histories.

Another way to bring us back for tomorrow's issue is to hype everything into a crisis or a tragedy. Crisis and tragedy are the meat and potatoes of journalism. Tragedies are more final—someone died. Crises are more fun—they are still going on. As the news makes us jaded, we need higher levels of excitement, bigger doses of stimulant.

The next time you see the word *crisis* on the front page (tomorrow), think what the word actually means. *Crisis* means a crossroads, a point of decision, a turning point where history may take a new direction. Can you remember the John Tower crisis? It was on the front page for several weeks, which is a long time in news consciousness. We waited to see whether the Senate would bow to President Bush's wish to appoint him defense secretary or to a puritanical public's wish to punish him for his moral deficiencies. Tower didn't get confirmed. Nothing else happened that I recall.

Tragedies are crises in which someone gets hurt. Actually, *tragedy* is not usually an accurate word, if you go by its technical meaning. *Disaster* might be better. Even *disaster* is usually over-dramatic, as in the "Three Mile Island disaster." No one died there. There were no measurable health effects (if I can believe later journalistic reports). It stopped the approval of new nuclear-power plants, which may or may not have been a disaster. So all the media really meant was the "Three Mile Island scare." That would be more accurate, but it might make it sound too much like part of our entertainment culture. We want scary news just like we want scary movies, but we like to think that the news is more real or more serious.

Editors have a saying: If it bleeds, it leads. Plane crashes always lead; they are scarier than a hundred car wrecks. If we got our news monthly in accounts with some claim to conclusiveness, plane crashes would only be mentioned along with the nation's traffic-death totals. That is because the point of monthly reports would be to inform. The point of news is to excite. If the news wasn't scary, we would lose interest. And how does this affect our judgment? Given the greater risk of dying on the highways than in the skies, it would be dumb to let the news scare us into driving instead. In general it would encourage better judgment to use the word *episode* instead of *crisis, death* instead of *tragedy* and *loss* instead of *disaster.* But those words may be too dull, too real, to sell the product.

The Dominance of Bad News
One of the best ways to keep us coming back is for journalists to start a fight. We'll say more about this when we get to what news does to our political life. But have you noticed how the good news

is followed immediately by the bad news? The good news might be that government economic indicators show an increase in productivity, but that is only due to an increase in orders. Unemployment declined, but this is considered only a seasonal adjustment. Congress's compromise budget saw a cut in military spending, but this will be devastating to many local economies.

Always a downside. We could call it double-entry news reporting. The new budget shows a decline in the deficit but not as great as had been hoped for. Housing starts were up, but that threatens to raise interest rates. Interest rates go down, but that will affect all those living on investment income.

It might seem like this is a mark of sophistication—looking beyond the obvious. But try turning that practice around. Try to imagine the news matching every report of bad news with its silver lining: "Unemployment rose last month; this is expected to ease inflationary pressures." "Slower growth this month will mean less pollution, less overtime work and therefore more time for us to do what is important in life." Things don't work that way in news. Good news needs to be tempered. Bad news stands alone, because worrying sells newspapers. If we were allowed to get complacent about the future, we would lose interest in the news and maybe let our subscription lapse.

Nursing Ambiguity

Another way of starting a fight is by creating ambiguity. Take the word *cut*, as in "budget cut." *Cut* is a short word that fits easily into headlines. Better still, it can confuse and worry us, to perk up our interest. When we read that there will be "cuts" in the government budget for X, it would be natural to assume that this means there will be less money for X next year than there was this year. But it almost never really means that. Governments just don't operate that way. Actually, *cut* can mean a number of things. Sometimes it means a decrease from present spending levels when inflation is taken into account. Sometimes it means a slower rise in an already rising trend. It can mean a decrease when adjusted for the growth of the relevant population. Or it can just mean some reduction of earlier projections, or proposals, for increased spending.

I'm looking at an article from the *Washington Post* (November 25, 1988) that uses the word *cut* in reference to Medicare (a hot-button issue) fourteen times. In this case it does *not* mean less money in the future. Buried in the fine print is the explanation that it means "compared with what would be spent if current law remains in effect and if increases were made to account for inflation and population change." That didn't fit into the headline, which reads "Bush Expected to Support Cuts in Medicare." Inside the paper one discovers that the rise in Medicare was being limited to 3.7 percent.

Freeze and *current levels* are ambiguous in just the same way, so it is conceivable that newswriters could call the same thing an increase or a freeze or a cut, as it suits their purposes. The saying around Washington, D.C., is that it is the only town where someone can ask for a $10,000 raise and when offered $5,000 complain that his salary is being cut by $5,000. Journalists headline "cuts" to get us on edge and make us anxious to see tomorrow's paper. There is no avoiding exaggeration and imprecision if we're going to turn each day into news. So headlines get bigger, stories get littler, words get shorter, brains get smaller.

A variation on the theme of manufactured conflict has to do with the names that newspeople assign to things. Let us say that a proposal before the legislature is called the Clean Water Bill in a string of news stories. Readers might naturally assume that such an enactment was intended to produce clean water. In fact, it might be for the purpose of building unnecessary dams. But it would be a brave governor who would veto something that the news had labeled the Clean Water Bill. Of course, it would be a mistake to assume that the reporters have actually read the bill to see why it might be opposed in the interests of the environment, thrift or any of a number of decent motives.

In 1990 something called the Civil Rights Bill was much in the news. President Bush tried to change the public's name for that legislation to the Racial Quota Bill to justify his intended veto. But he didn't own a newspaper, and editors—not mere presidents—decide these names. Similarly, his "defense budgets"—which could be expected to pay for bullets and such—might be spent largely on generals' pensions, landscaping military headquarters and maintaining the aerospace industry in case we need it later. The labels are there to confuse us by making things simple. Referring to the bills by their numbers might be less misleading.

The most irritating way newswriters set the news pot boiling is simply to keep up a confrontational tone. It often sounds as if writers are complaining even when there is nothing to complain about. Bruce McCall wrote a *New Yorker* parody of this style, and a couple of paragraphs will give you the idea.

> The rickety old bus full of bawling infants and caged chickens never comes; we must take a gleaming new one instead. There is no time to quibble. We have come to a wide river, and no ferryboat is available to take us across. Instead, government engineers have thrown a bridge of sorts across from the near to the far bank. It is just four lanes wide, and only a shoulder-high concrete retaining wall, a wire fence, and a few iron stanchions on either side prevent wayward vehicles or pedestrians from plunging into the rapids below. The bus makes the two-thousand-foot crossing in thirty seconds that seem like half a minute. Yet there is no cheering from the passengers as we finally gain firm ground on the other side.

The story of "Jack" (real name: John) typifies life as it is lived today in this, the new Canada. He had no choice after graduating from elementary school but to attend high school, and after high school no choice but to attend university, and after university no choice but to go to work. "It's the system," he confides, without evident bitterness. Jack is twenty-eight.[2]

One can't help thinking that McCall must have been remembering old news stories. What is irritating these reporters? Is it just the demands of their enterprise? Is this what it takes to keep us off balance?

So far we've been talking about distortions that reporters adopt innocently and unconsciously. But recently the industry has become increasingly open to using deception for the sake of sales. It seems strange to have actual debate over whether TV newspeople should be allowed to reenact "events" for their broadcasts so that we can imagine we are watching news unfold. Also our courts have ruled that a print journalist may make up "quotes" and attribute them to public figures if the quote reflects their general positions in the judgment of the reporter. It would be nice if in a culture of lies—by advertisers, public relations personnel, politicians, developers, reforming ideologues—the news were an oasis of truth. But the demands of the industry pushes the limits.

News Reports on Itself
It is in the nature of excitement that it must be maintained continuously, renewed every day. And when all else fails, the news can report on itself. On a slow news day we may have features on whether the press is becoming too intrusive, too powerful or too unfair, or whether it's being threatened by would-be censors. There are even stories on whether the news is reporting on itself too much. I saw one report during the 1988 political campaign that there were

more than a hundred network news stories on the role of the press in that election.

The public seems to have accepted this narcissism. Take Miss Winter Haven of 1988, a budding journalist competing in the Florida State Beauty Pageant, who enthused, "I've found that the real joy of reporting is not just communicating and stirring emotions in people, but being a catalyst for change and making things happen."[3] Stirring emotions and making things happen used to be the definition of demagoguery. She was on to something, though. Daily news has a dynamic that drives it past its ostensible purpose of providing a window on the world. It cannot help becoming creative in the manner Miss Winter Haven pines for. No reporter is satisfied to frame our view when he or she might fill the screen.

This is just another way of saying that news has a way of crowding everything else out and becoming the only reality. My town had an instance of this recently in the fortunes of our university's FM station. A few years ago one could tune in to this station at any time of day and hear the world's greatest music in all of its fantastic variety. The station managers got bored with this. It wasn't enough to listen to someone else's creativity when they had some of their own to share. They weren't satisfied with providing a music service; they wanted to run a real radio station. So they began to speak of "development." Developing the station turned out to mean reducing the time for music and increasing the amount of talk. Exciting talk didn't mean Dylan Thomas reading great poetry, of course. It meant news and interviewing those who are in the news. So the station managers applied for government grants to buy equipment so they could go out and collect this news. Government is always willing to support such things, because it knows that the news will magnify its importance.

Once the station managers had the equipment, they wanted to use it. There's no sense in sitting around waiting for something to happen. That might take months in a town like ours. They had to be aggressive, so they set aside more and more time for newscasting and then created the news to fill it. The results are unbelievably puerile. Now when you tune in to that station you more than likely will hear someone talking. Beethoven's trios have been traded for reports on the alleged procurement scandal in the fire department.

I was on a citizens' advisory committee for the station at the time. A fellow member, a political groupie, said that she could always play records if she wanted to hear music, but where else could she get the news "in depth"? At that time the station had a modest collection of about twenty thousand records; her personal record library may have numbered something around forty. I suppose she was tired of them, whereas the news seemed new every day. Some people feel the opposite—they find Chopin fresh every day, whereas news stories seem stale the first time you hear them.

Dead on Arrival

Despite the creativity that goes into news reporting, the media put out a product that is dead on arrival. Try this simple test. Go to your public library or attic or someplace that keeps old newspapers, and find one from several years back. See how it affects you. Does it strike you as a masterpiece? Is it something that you could admire day after day without exhausting its statement? Would a tape of local news, say twenty years old, compare with the delight of some popular song from that time? Or will it seem quaint, naive, embarrassing? The embarrassment comes from being reminded that you were once agog about something that turned out to be so trivial.

I don't begrudge the news to those who crave it. The point of my story about the radio station is that there were dozens of other stations that aired news but none that played culture. Why does our society neglect history and philosophy and science and the arts and take in *only* the news? Do we think somehow that we're getting a digest of all the rest in those news reports?

One would think that anything so ephemeral would have a hard time competing with great literature and thought. Quite the reverse. We have bought the idea that we've got to deal with the news first and then get to the rest if there is time left over. I would not deny that some things in the news actually turned out to be historically important. But of the tens of thousands of newspapers you have read, how many are you saving for your grandchildren? The ones announcing the dropping of the atom bomb on Japan, the attack on Pearl Harbor, the discovery of penicillin, President Kennedy's or Martin Luther King Jr.'s assassination or President Nixon's resignation? Yet even those papers don't explain the importance of those events; they only give a sense of their immediacy and excitement. Most old papers will just seem like filler, the stuffing from empty lives.

In an article in the *New York Times* on December 15, 1995, Hilton Kramer remembered having an editor at the *Times* who always opened editorial meetings with "So what's new?" One day an exasperated Kramer was ready for him and blurted out, "There's absolutely nothing new this week." The editor, knocked off stride for only a second, responded, "Is that a trend?" This is a parable for our time, in which we are determined to know only what is new and nothing about the world of thought in which the new will find its place.

BUT FIRST, THESE HEADLINES

• *New York Times*, **February 16, 1989: "A Latin Peace Plan Not So Broad: Ball in Nicaragua's Court"**

• *Financial Times*, **same day: "Central American Peace Plan Puts Ball Back in U.S. Court"**

• *San Francisco Chronicle*, **May 25, 1989: "West Pointers Hiss Quayle"**

• *San Jose Mercury*, **same day: "Cadets Ignore Controversy over Quayle"**

• *Boston Globe*, **January 1, 1989: "After 20 Years, Anti-snob Zoning Found Ineffective"**

• **Same paper, January 2, 1989: "Zoning Law Weathers Conflict: After 18 Years, Mass. Anti-snob Rule Called a Success"**

How about a warning label on the news that reads "This product has been shown to cause dizziness and memory loss"?

3

Being Informed
Versus
Being Wise

I have already alluded to the fact that intellectuals, of all people, seem the most addicted to news and the proudest of being "informed." How can I be arguing, then, that news makes us dumb? How can getting information on a daily basis interfere with the higher mental processes? Does being informed differ from being *wise*—an old-fashioned word for seeing things in their widest context?

For starters, when people say that the news keeps them "informed," we can presume that they mean they are learning about the most significant events from all around the world. And further, the idea of being objectively informed implies that people in different countries would find some agreement in listing the most important events. They might not be in perfect agreement, but if it makes any sense to speak of "world news," it ought to look pretty similar from wherever one stands on the globe.

On April 11, 1994, *Time* listed the top four stories on the leading TV networks in eleven different countries for March 29, 1994. I don't know why they did this, since it called their whole enterprise into question. If being informed is meaningful, the eleven networks should have agreed on the stories or on most of them. Or at least on *some* of them. There could be as few as four stories heading the news in all the countries. If we allowed one domestic story per country among the top four, that would make eleven plus three common stories, or fourteen in all. If there were absolutely no agreement on the significant news from around the world, there would be eleven times four, or forty-four.

How many stories would you guess were listed? There were forty-two. Japan and Britain shared one story, as did Australia and South Africa. So you could think of yourself as "informed" in the United States while being pretty much out of it in Mexico, Brazil, India, Kenya, Egypt, Australia, South Africa, Japan, Britain and Russia. Who is really informed, then? Do we just assume that *we* are informed, while all these other countries have their heads in the sand? In fact, all of the top U.S. stories that day were domestic.

Now you might say, "Of course people want to read more about their own corner of the world than about all those other countries." I entirely agree. But we should be honest enough to admit that we do not even begin to be informed about "the world." We may be following just three foreign stories from among hundreds, probably thousands, of stories that the industry might have served up for us.

Let's say you are really serious about staying informed, so you take four important newspapers and spend hours every day getting through them all, like Michael Douglas does. Would that do it? The CIA comprises about twenty thousand people—the population of a whole town—who collectively try to keep up to date with 180-plus countries. They read *all* the important newspapers as well as all their other sources of information. Are they getting the job done? Ironically, intellectuals are precisely the people who seem to have the least respect for the CIA and treat it as a joke. Where does that leave them, with their paltry four papers?

Being "Informed" Is Impossible

Let's face it. There is simply no way to be "informed" in the sense that we imagine. If you stopped reading the paper tomorrow, you would not suddenly become uninformed; you are already uninformed about anything as big as "the world." You learn this when you actually visit one of those 180-plus countries. Travel helps you realize that your previous notion of being informed was simply infantile.

Stopping this pretense would mark a gain in realism. If we used the time we spend sampling news product to read something more substantial we would start becoming informed—about a few things, anyway. We would be admitting that not one of us is God, and that would be a big blow to people who thought that their news consumption made them effectively omniscient.

This pinhole notion of "the world" is a fantasy. It is equivalent to the mythological cosmos that earlier civilizations imagined, except that theirs didn't deconstruct itself every day. (We'll come back to this point later.)

It turns out that being informed really means knowing what the people around you are talking about. Our reality is the news, not the world. It is true that we need topics to talk about if we are to have civilized society. But those talking points don't need to come from news product. If you really want to go upscale, there are infinitely more important things to talk about than the plane crashes, shooting rampages and party bickering that fill the news—philosophical and religious questions, science and social values, for example.

We ignore these topics because the news ignores them. And the news ignores them because they wouldn't bring us back for more tomorrow. The more successful the answers, the less we will have to revisit the question again. News specializes in questions we will never be able to answer conclusively—not because they are so big but because they aren't real questions.

When we don't visit our most basic beliefs, our thinking becomes shallow. The reason that old newspapers and magazines often seem childish is that they are full of ideology instead of thought. That is, they just tell us what was once fashionable to think. Of course we all imagine that we are thinking for ourselves. But when we are suddenly reminded of what we used to think, we realize that we change our ideas like we change our hats. We weren't argued out of those old ideas; we just haven't heard them in a while. So reading a stack of old papers is nothing like rereading a classic novel, for example. We might find the novel *more* striking the second time around, whereas what passed for ideas in the newspapers may now seem juvenile.

Once again, daily publication is to blame. There is no extended thinking in news reports because it takes too much space to explain something. We find statements rather than arguments, and this has a serious effect on our minds. If news constitutes all of our reading, we fall into the habit of thinking that opinions are the same as thoughts. The news alludes to a debate but can only show us a clash of opinions. As a result, we short-circuit discussion by falling back on polls. Polls have replaced debate in news reporting because they don't need to be explained. A poll just counts heads; it doesn't tell us what is inside them. But it may be that the smaller number of heads contain the best thinking on the subject at hand. Daily news has a way of making us forget that there is any thinking going on, implying that all positions spring out of nowhere—the expression of someone's vested interests.

The most that news can do to introduce a little sophistication is to offer quotes from opposing sides. This always means reporting on two extremes with the implication that the truth must lie in the middle. But there is no reason to think this is justified. The truth might lie at or even beyond one of those extremes.

Absolute Relativism

Let me test you on this point. Are you wary of the term *truth* in a discussion like this? Nothing is more common nowadays than to have someone interrupt a serious discussion with the objection "Who's to say what the truth is anyway?" or "If that's your opinion, that's fine for you." Why do we say this? Nobody in their innermost heart believes that standards of truth are unreal. Academics, who often describe themselves as relativists, would lose their authoritative, elite position if relativism were taken seriously, and their students would have to grade themselves. But a flippant relativism has become a habit with us, a habit encouraged by the "evenhandedness" of the news.

If we say, "There is no absolute truth," we expect others to accept this as a true statement—or else what good is it? So whereas a true relativism is self-canceling, the news version of relativism is very dogmatic. Skepticism is the creed of the news, if that is not a contradiction. One might think that the evenhandedness of news means a respect for everyone's opinion. Actually, it means undermining whatever is stated too emphatically by reporting that there are those who disagree. Maybe this is our idea of being modest or democratic.

We argue our great social issues badly because we hold the idea that all "viewpoints" are somehow equal. The sketchiness of news coverage encourages this notion. We are so used to its juggling approach to ideas that we have lost the patience and the humility to submit our opinions to true argumentation. Is abortion murder? How would one decide? Should we try to deduce an answer from philosophical principles or from our feelings or from polls? How could we consider theological insights? We wouldn't know how to begin to answer. What is compelling about philosophical principles, for instance?

Sometimes newspeople will appeal to experts, as in "some

experts believe . . ." This is a step in the right direction, because there are people who have devoted real attention to most of our issues. But there won't be space in the story for the experts to tell us why they believe what they do, which is vital. And what about the other experts, who may not "believe . . ." Come to think of it, how do newspeople know an expert when they see one? Even experts can't always agree on who the other experts are.

In the chapter on science we will return to the question of how daily news deals with experts—by predigesting them for us. For the moment I will only remind you that we still have deep thinkers among us. They are pretty much ignored by reporters, though. What would be the point of calling on them if they can't sum up their philosophical position on the current subject in a sound bite? If a Nobel Prize were given for philosophy, we would at least know the winners' names, for news is good at giving us such irrelevant information. But the news would probably be more interested in their hobbies than their ideas.

When Allan Bloom wrote *The Closing of the American Mind*, he made his story a lot more complicated than it had to be. The sad state of our nation's intellectual life has less to do with wayward philosophical movements than with a simple fixation on the moment. Of course Bloom was right to have been concerned with a society that is so intellectually feeble. There has been a serious decay of our ability to relate our ideas to each other in a logical manner and to relate our institutions to each other in a supportive way and to relate different rights so as to create justice. But all of these failures may simply stem from consuming all ideas daily.

Take, for example, Bloom's issue of "values." Actually we have plenty of values. Our problem is that we don't have any agreed *scale* of values. You need a scale of values, a ranking, so that you can argue logically about which values should override others. Some have to be more basic than others, or they will all be a jumble.

Traditional cultures have scales of values, but in a news culture the news makes every value absolute—for the time being. *Absolute* here means that all other values become relative to and subordinate to that one. The news alerts us to a problem that some group with whom we can all sympathize is having. There is never space or time, however, to assess that group's needs against other demands on the treasury or law enforcement resources, or to weigh its rights against those of groups that might be thrown in to competition. Rather, the news absolutizes a particular group or value—for the moment.

In our secular culture we can absolutize any value we want—a new one every week. It is the sort of thing that comes naturally to news reporting. Odd, isn't it, that a medium that has such a relativizing effect on our mental activity finds itself absolutizing values this way? But it's only temporary. There will be another paper tomorrow with something else to wring our hearts. The news never needs to argue us out of a former concern or into another. Daily publication has conditioned us to forget last week's concern. Concentrating on the news has trained us to live in an absolute present.

If the news makes us scatterbrained, what would the opposite of news be? Meditation, I suppose. Imagine that one day you opened your newspaper and found just one word in the whole paper. One word, like

charm

What's this? You've paid for news and set aside fifteen minutes for it. You want to be plugged in socially. Are you angry or anxious about being left in the dark? Or are you delighted to think that the world has finally found the peace to consider and concentrate on something like

charm

It's a wonderful word, when you stop to think about it. Turn it around in your mind to see all its facets. That fifteen minutes could be an oasis in your normal, driven existence. You might consider changing your subscription to a daily meditation service that would provide words like *alive* or even *green.* Considering any of them for fifteen minutes could deepen the mystery of your existence. In the time you now spend letting the news upset you, in preparation for a busy day, you could open your awareness to something much closer to or even inside you.

Our addiction to news is keeping meditation from sweeping the country. Of course if meditation caught on, we would find the periodical publishers joining in. *Timely Meditations* (Metro Edition) would offer words like

VIOLATION

That would have the desired effect, getting our anxieties pumping first thing in the morning. In fact, *violation* would work so well that they might repeat it the next day.

Was the Holocaust a News Event?
If I sound escapist, remember that the world of the news represents

an infinitesimally tiny fraction of reality, and it does not even pretend to visit the big questions. There is a good example of this failure in the original news coverage of the Holocaust. In an interesting study of this episode Professor Barbie Zelizer shows how "words failed" to convey a fraction of what the initial reporters wanted to say about what they had seen in the death camps.[1] The reporters fell back on photographs, which gave the event a larger importance. But editors never figured out how to use these pictures journalistically, with proper regard to their position in time, place and so on. The photos became "universal" symbols, and Zelizer describes the newspeople's uneasiness about using them.

It seems to me that this shows something hopeful about those editors but sad about their profession. They sensed that this "event" was too big for a news treatment. The whole notion of "events" shows the limits of daily reporting, which has to use and dispose of stories and move on. Words didn't fail the editors; news discourse did. The Holocaust was a religious or "mythic" episode in the sense that it revealed something ultimate, something Zelizer quite properly calls "human depravity." She quotes one of the newspeople, E. Z. Dimitman, who said at the time that

a man who has been on major newspaper desks for nearly 20 years knows how quickly John Q. Public forgets. When the man happens to be one of the small group of American editors chosen to inspect Nazi concentration camps while the horror was still fresh, he has extra reason to fear this short memory. E. Z. Dimitman saw Buchenwald and Dachau and he will see them all his life. He wants American newspapers to help make sure we do not forget.[2]

Unfortunately, helping us "not forget" is not a job the news is good at. News cuts everything down to the same size so that we can dispose of it and move on to another installment tomorrow. What the world needed was to stop and just gape at this enormity. Photos helped, particularly when they didn't come with the little tags that gave the names, dates and places of a news report. But the news industry couldn't declare a suspension of schedules while we got in touch with eternal sources of wonder and repentance. It had to move on. Thereby the news may have helped create the kind of mentality that can deny the "event" later. For how can moderns believe anything that is too big for the news frame? We would need a historical consciousness to do that.

News and the Eternal

Religion has traditionally been the arena in which we have entertained the biggest questions. Maybe you've wondered why our society seems divided between those who spend Sunday morning going to church and those who spend it plowing through the Sunday paper. You may even have suspected that there is some incompatibility here, some spiritual opposition between religion and news.

There is. News and religion are natural antagonists. News is only aware of change, while religion tries to concentrate on the eternal, even within change. The whole idea of news—that for every 24-hour period there is an hour's worth of reports that require our attention—would be considered by any of the world's major religions a sign of being spiritually lost. Even a historian wouldn't need more than an hour to lecture on several years of human history. Any saint would understand that even that much would distract us from an understanding of our being. The things that nourish that sense of being (another great word) are music, philosophy, art, science, dance, literature—not reports *about* these things; much less the reports of wars, business, politics and other mischief. Anthropologically speaking, all those arts were born of religious experience, as part of the celebration of life and the powers behind our lives. Sociologically speaking, all of them are now in danger as news crowds out anything reflective.

The antagonism between religion and news is quite unconscious. Newspeople do not recognize any conflict with religion as such. But we've all noticed that the religious leaders who get into the news are pretty disreputable types. This should tell us something about the nature of news. Religion becomes the subject of the news when it has not been behaving itself. News coverage of religion quite naturally tends toward stories about celebrity evangelists who are caught in a scandal. Or the news will point up the religious dimensions of current conflicts and even wars. This is perfectly proper, given the nature of news. There cannot be news about people in the grip of the eternal.

Some religious leaders these days have accepted a news outlook to the extent that they want to use the media to change the world— the world of the news, that is. They think that the power of news to shape our minds ought to be captured for religion, to give God some leverage over his world. They must not understand how religion itself changes when it is given a news treatment.

In 1992 six religion editors were asked to list the top religious stories of the previous year. What exactly is a religious story? The editors thought they were being asked what difference religion made politically, so they listed various religious debates that promised some political fallout. Historically, that is never how spiritual movements have started. Great spiritual movements, like the civil rights movement, are only noticed by newspeople when they have become political.

So religious news doesn't go to the heart of religion. There could be reports of what percentage of all charitable giving came through religious as opposed to nonreligious organizations or reports of how many people attended services last Sunday. Yet even that would tell us nothing of how broken spirits were healed or families were blessed. These things aren't news, but that doesn't make them unreal. Newspeople never claimed that they discussed everything important, but unfortunately that assumption has been made by the rest of us. So as our attention becomes more and more riveted to daily reports, the ultimate concerns of life get less of our attention. What creates upset is news; what creates faith and hope is something else.

The last theological issue that got headlines was the controversy over the slogan "God is dead." Those theologians who rallied around this statement must have chosen the slogan to make the news. It fit into a lot of headlines. But they did not get their point across. How could they, given the constraints of daily publishing? It was all a success from the media's standpoint, of course: it sold a lot of magazines.

Not only will you never learn anything about religion by reading the news, you will not learn anything real about religious institutions either. Remember how it goes? Reporters are sent to cover some denomination's annual assembly, while the participants hope to have as quiet a meeting as possible and make no news in the process. The reporters are not easily put off. They look over the agenda and find that one of the five study groups—the one on the church in the world—has a task force on social concerns (one of three task forces) that has a committee on community relations (one of four committees) with a subcommittee on homosexuality in the church. Another study group (on ministry) has a task force on mission whose committee on worship includes a subcommittee on gender-specific terminology in the liturgy. Guess what the news from this assembly will concentrate on. And we wonder, why are the churches so preoccupied with sex?

The natural antagonism between news and religion came near to surfacing in the news coverage of Martin Scorsese's movie *The Last Temptation of Christ.* Scores of press and TV interviews concentrated on the inflammatory response of one bizarre minister of a small Los Angeles congregation to the exclusion of less colorful Christian spokespeople. Meanwhile media reviewers suggested that there was nothing irreverent about the film. Movie critic Michael Medved attended the prerelease screenings of the movie with his fellow critics and noted that they "began snickering, hooting, and laughing aloud midway through the picture. . . . I was therefore amazed and appalled in the days that followed at the generally respectful—even reverential—tone that so many of my colleagues adopted in their reviews." When he confronted one critic who had snorted the loudest during the screening yet later wrote a glowing review of the movie, the man admitted, "I know the picture's a dog. We both know that, and probably Scorsese knows it, too. But with all the Christian crazies shooting at him from every direction, I'm not going to knock him in public. . . . People would associate me with Falwell."[3] To this film critic, *Christian* is probably synonymous with *crazy*.

For a large part of the population, religion is a major part of life. But news about religion cannot get to its essence—irrespective of what a reporter's sympathies might be. The culture wars in general are about whether any aspect of culture can be viewed as really and truly settled, as absolute in the sense that one's religion is taken to be absolute. The news cannot admit any such conclusion. Tomorrow must have a new edition, and that edition must suggest that there is a new world out there. So what has always seemed reasonable, natural or good must be challenged not just now and then but constantly.

The Sunday paper includes sections on the things that really matter, like work, relaxation, family and religion. Editors have a hard time making news out of them, but if you find yourself drawn to those features more than to the hard news, it may say something good about you.

Every so often some pundit suggests that religion may be having a quiet resurgence. Usually this seems like wishful thinking, a revulsion against the binge of irresponsibility and indulgence that we call individualism. But any well-wisher to religion will fervently hope that any such religious revival will never make the news. Can't you imagine how reports would go? The media will locate the "spokespeople" for this movement of the Spirit or perhaps create them. Those persons will play to the cameras and become less spontaneous, less real. They will learn the usual ways of getting media attention and try to squeeze their message into a slogan. That slogan will be bounced around until the industry senses that the public is losing interest. And so the renewal becomes a thing of the day and not of the Spirit.

Malcolm Muggeridge was a long-time journalist who came to repent this misspent life when he converted to Catholicism. He once ruefully admitted, "I've often thought . . . that if I'd been a journalist in the Holy Land at the time of our Lord's ministry, I should have spent my time looking into what was happening in Herod's court. I'd be wanting to sign up Salome for her exclusive memoirs, and finding out what Pilate was up to, and . . . I would have missed completely the most important event there ever was."[4]

Something has to be sacred, of course, and the news is now handling that side of things for us too. It has its own list of taboos: the First Amendment is the the first of all commandments. Censorship is blasphemy. But *real* blasphemy, if directed at the views of the majority, is almost a sacred duty. Charity means entertaining our customers. Because boredom is hell.

WHEN NEWS WAS ONLY PART OF
LIFE AND CULTURE

Ingenious philosophers tell you, perhaps, that the great work of the steam-engine is to create leisure for mankind. Do not believe them: it only creates a vacuum for eager thought to rush in. Even idleness is eager now—eager for amusement; prone to excursion-trains, art museums, periodical literature and exciting novels; prone even to scientific theorizing and cursory peeps through microscopes. Old Leisure was quite a different personage. He only read one newspaper, innocent of leaders [headlines], and was free from that periodicity of sensations which we call post-time [when the papers arrived]. He was a contemplative, rather stout gentleman, of excellent digestion; of quiet perceptions, undiseased by hypothesis; happy in his inability to know the causes of things, preferring the things themselves.

GEORGE ELIOT

4

How
News Schedules
Drive Our
Government

If I asked you to close your eyes and then said the word *government*, the image that would probably swim through your mind would be the U.S. Capitol dome. In earlier centuries the image would have been that of a court building. This difference marks one of the most fateful changes in history. Daily news helped cause this change, making problems that it now offers to help us solve.

During the nineteenth century Western societies began to look on government as a force for *changing* things. Before that time, government was supposed to *maintain* things. Courts were to enforce the laws and sometimes even the customs of a society, because people didn't like the idea that government could change the rules on them constantly. In the 1520s Christopher St. German, an English legal expert, wrote that any law that violated the *customs* of the English people would be null, or as we would now say, unconstitutional. Indeed some ancient societies had refused to have their laws written down, for how could you consider yourself a free person if there were too many laws to remember?

Things have changed. Around the time of the American and French revolutions, people began to sense that changes were needed and that government was the only tool big enough to make these changes. Many good things have followed from encouraging government to be a force for change—and many bad things. Centuries from now people may view the twentieth century as incomparably the most murderous in history—a time of ideological and world wars worse than any in the Dark Ages, of governments that slaughtered their own populations, of unprecedented levels of torture, homelessness, abandonment and environmental degradation. We are too fond of contrasting our privileged niche in our century with the most negative caricature of earlier ones.

I don't mean to blame daily publication for all the failings of this most disappointing of centuries. What I am saying is that the news industry has encouraged the assumption that ceaseless, churning change is the normal state of society and that it is the government's job to encourage it. Whereas people once wanted to keep government at arm's length so that society could manage itself, they now hope to harness government and use it to arrange other people more to their liking. When legislators go off to the state capital, what we expect of them is "productivity." We seem to want more laws every year—more change in our lives—like people who can't stand the new house they just built.

Daily news has doubtless been one of the most important causes of this revolution in thinking. News demands legislative productivity if for no other reason than to give the papers something to report. In return, editors encourage the view that news should focus mostly on our politicians. They fill up their pages by following politicians around and seeing everything in its political dimension.

Symbiosis of News and Politics

There is a truly symbiotic relationship between politics-as-movement and the news. If we thought our problems had suddenly been solved, it would be the end of the world for politicians and newspeople. So it suits both of them that every solution generates a new "problem." A number of writers have commented on this recently.

Peggy Noonan, having written news product for Dan Rather at CBS before moving over to the White House to write politics for President Reagan, was in a perfect position to observe the news-government-public relations complex. She later described the "dance" of politics with the media. In Washington, she said, the insiders' favorite TV program is the *McLaughlin Report,* where they might hear themselves mentioned. This is the program, you'll recall, where participants yell at each other in imitation of journalistic debate. Noonan worried about what she saw at the empty center of this news-politics complex. She warned her readers to "beware the politically obsessed. They are often bright and interesting, but they have something missing in their natures; there is a hole, an empty place, and they use politics to fill it up. It leaves them somehow misshapen."[1] Similarly, we could say that news fills up an empty space within us. Except it never really fills. We continue to ache to be filled with something more solid—something that we don't even know to look for anymore.

In the midst of the 1992 election *Time* did a piece entitled "Are the Media Too Liberal?" The question was whether reporters were, however unconsciously, favoring Clinton over Bush. The article was typically ambiguous, but buried in its shallows was one clear-eyed observation.

By far the biggest factor, however, is a variation on the one that is apparently motivating voters: a simple yearning for change. After a dozen years of Republican rule, journalists hunger for new battles, new issues, above all new faces. A change in ruling party always energizes politics and boosts stories to the front page or the opening of the newscast. Says a *Washington Post* reporter: "God, I hope Bush doesn't get re-elected. It'll be so boring: no fresh ideas, the same old people running the show and more Capitol Hill gridlock. A Clinton Administration would be a much better story." In all likelihood, four years from now the same reporters will turn on Clinton with the same jaded ferocity.[2]

The *New Republic* made similar comments about the politicians involved in all this.

> The ambitious members of Congress care much more about getting on television than they do about going to hunting lodges and golf courses with lobbyists . . . or pursuing an ideological agenda. . . . When publicity is the coin of the realm in Washington, scandals are, in effect, the mint. Whenever another "gate" hits Washington, the sense of communal joy is almost palpable. The nation's usually wandering attention is firmly fixed on the capital, which confirms the correctness of the career decisions made by thousands of student-body presidents who moved there on the assumption that Washington is the center of the world.[3]

So we have entered a stage in which politics is equated with commotion. Perhaps this tossing and turning is not the natural state of a healthy society, but we accept it—maybe because we think it will mean changing other people's lives rather than our own.

Are the Media Liberal?

Now I bet you know what's coming. It sounds like I'm going to say that those who welcome politics-as-movement and a powerful news industry are what we call "liberals." Stay with me for a minute.

You're right. I am saying that news is liberal by its very nature. We may speak of "conservative newspapers," but that only reveals a confusion in our thinking. Anyone who publishes a daily paper has accepted the idea that change is the really important feature of life, and this is not a conservative sentiment. Such a publisher would be only *comparatively* conservative, on the more stodgy wing of our liberal society. He or she might be reactionary but not really conservative.

Daily news is liberal by its very nature because the emphasis is on "liberty" and therefore on change and on testing authority. The conservative emphasis is on "conserving," on order and stability, and on honoring authority.

Liberalism creates movement, and therefore it is the subject of periodical news. Conservatism retards movement, and that is not appreciated by the news.

The Left makes news and needs daily news to help it drive change. The Right feels threatened by a fascination with news; it expresses itself instead in works of piety and solidarity.

So which side should we be on? Why must we choose one or the other? A healthy society needs both liberty and order, change and stability. The problem is our present addiction to change—as if it were good in and of itself. In 1992 presidential candidate Bill Clinton did not think that a call for "change" required any justification or explanation as a political slogan. In fact, his administration has proved to be a very moderate one, although we seem to want to imagine we are in a whirl of change.

Nature tends to divide us into two camps, *movement* and *stability,* and our liberal and conservative parties reflect that division. One party comes up with ideas; the other party challenges those ideas. Liberals see the glass as half empty and hope to see it filled. Conservatives see the glass as at least half full and want to be careful not to spill any. Surely we need both sides. Good ideas are hard to come by; questioning them helps our humility. But as long as periodical information dominates our outlook on the world and on our lives, the forces for stability are at an insuperable disadvantage.

The fact that conservatives often start newspapers just shows how little they understand the situation. If their papers are going to be published periodically, then change is going to be their subject. They may have thought that their papers could counteract the forces of mindless change, but in the end they will also encourage a politics of movement. Real journalists will side with a party of change not necessarily because it is more compassionate but because it is more attuned to the news.

The one thing that conservative politicians can do in the media is serve as villains. Having both bad guys and good guys heightens public interest, so in this way Republicans are vital to the news— none more so than Senator Jesse Helms. He appears to be trying to win the award for blocking the most legislation each year, which might have been applauded more by the Founding Fathers than it is today. For nowadays journalists see no irony in separating our politicians into "the obstructionists" and "the serious legislators," as *Time* put it on October 10, 1994. Serious legislators are those who are serious about making news.

Movement Politics

As an example of the politics-as-movement mentality, one might take Democratic-party figure Robert Strauss, who told a *Time* reporter (March 14, 1988) that "I would be a great President. I know how to move this country." The reporter did not ask, "Move it where?" Ever since John Kennedy called the stability of the Eisenhower years into question, we have bought into the notion that presidents are supposed to "get the country moving again." Surprisingly, the man who was actually elected president in 1988 was not

Strauss but George Bush, who promised only more of the same.

The news did not let President Bush rest, however. Shortly into his administration the media went through the new ritual of taking stock of the president's accomplishments in "the first hundred days"—three months and small change. Nothing very dramatic had happened in Washington in that amount of time. This was, if I understood him correctly, what Bush's campaign had been about. But it did nothing to accommodate the news industry. And so I quote the *New Republic,* May 8, 1989: "As I sit down to write this, George Bush has in fact been president of the United States for exactly 89 days. But the exigencies of magazine publishing—'lead time,' we call it—require the gun to be jumped. Of course, Bush still has 11 days to pull off some dazzling feat." The editor had no choice, you see. He was required to give his one-hundred-day assessment early. Why, we may wonder, must government march to any such beat?

Even more amazing was Bush's response in trying to justify those first three months. The newspeople, who are always snapping at a president's heels, actually got him to tote up his accomplishments. He didn't want to be seen as losing "momentum." Bush understood that the news requires someone to lead the parade. Those who actually voted for Bush must have wanted an administrator rather than a leader, but news can't report on simple administration unless it is unusually clumsy or crooked. It isn't daily. And Bush didn't know the people who voted for him as well as he knew those newsmen.

Beyond its concentration on government, the news creates a concentration on the presidency. This sharpens the focus on policy, rather than administration, on leadership and on change. Newspeople hound presidents to give us leadership. And so we have the growth of the "imperial presidency" that editors lament.

In the exceptional autumn of 1989, when there was, briefly, some point in watching daily news, the communist states couldn't collapse quickly enough for the news. If you recall, the papers were frantically asking why our leaders were not out in front of those changes. *Why haven't they responded to the Soviet leaders' latest helpless, unilateral giveaway offer? Why haven't they developed a plan to reunify Germany? Why isn't someone taking control?*

Lest you think only liberals pine for leadership and movement, consider the right-wing journalists of that same period. Just before the collapse of Soviet power in Angola, Ethiopia, Nicaragua, the Middle East, Afghanistan and Eastern Europe, conservative journalists wrote hand-wringing articles about how the State Department was about to "lose" all those places. They thought the government was "drifting" just when a strong hand was needed at the helm. This was just before our diplomats watched, slack-jawed, as the dominos fell all around them. (Of course, we still don't know *what* has been won. Truth is the offspring of time, not of news.)

The news has focused our minds to a very sharp point—on our political activities and especially on our leader. You cannot imagine an evening news program in which the president is not mentioned. There was a time when we turned to government as a last resort for those jobs that only a government could do. Politicizing an issue used to be considered a sign of failure; society had proved unable to settle it by more natural means, that is, by agreement rather than by power. Now officials rush to take a position on the next big issue, proving their leadership abilities and making sure we don't forget their names.

David Halberstam's book *The Powers That Be* traces the way in which American politicians and the press have come to view each other as the only reality. He describes how John Kennedy loved to chat with almost anybody who dropped by the White House until the evening news came on, when no one was allowed to make a peep. "It was sacred," Halberstam says. "He put more concentration into watching the news than into almost anything else, you could watch with him but you could not talk. . . . Perhaps it was not reality and perhaps it was not even good journalism, *but it was what the country perceived as reality* and thus in a way was closer to reality than reality itself."[4]

More real than reality? No wonder Kennedy is still so popular with the press. By contrast, Ronald Reagan set out to prove that the country didn't really need a leader—maybe didn't even need a president, except to keep more meddlesome people out of the position. Understandably, he was not a favorite with newspeople. The 1980s were a very good time for the country in many respects, but President Reagan was not forgiven for the fact that the good things happened without enough regard to the conventional rituals of "leadership." So the good news (sustained economic growth that tamed tremendous inflation, falling crime rates, the collapse of regimes in the Philippines and Haiti that had long been irritants, tax reform and tax reduction, peaceful victory in a forty-year-old cold war) was in the news version obliterated by concentrating on the downside (increasing deficits, crumbling cities, widespread drug dependency, the spread of AIDS, neglected children). It bears remembering what newspeople in 1980 predicted would be the result of a Reagan presidential victory—war, higher taxes and economic depression. These same people are still making predictions. I'm sure they are glad that old newspapers are being recycled instead of reread.

Reagan's unpopularity with the press is instructive. As the fourth branch of government, the press insists that we take government seriously. How could we take seriously a president who took naps? Journalists might admit that the Reagan years were good for some people in some ways—as was indicated by our very unusual step in electing his vice president after him. But they would argue that Reagan himself wasn't responsible for the good things. He was just lucky. That is disturbing to a believer in the notion that "government saves." If we were to give up this faith, the sale of news would plummet. If one believed that human affairs are largely out of human control, it would make a mockery of news. News has to have personality to mask the randomness of life. In short, news has to anthropomorphize developments and create a myth of the world's process—a myth in which someone is in control. Someone we can blame.

Real political insiders must understand how little sense the political world makes. They must be amused to see how journalists try to make a simple human story out of the political circus. Naturally they are curious about how the news is "playing" something they are involved in, but only because they want to know what the public is going to think about it.

News as Sleeping Watchdog
Political insiders also know how much of the government is in the hands of bureaucrats who never appear in the news. Bureaucrats are unlike politicians in that they do not *want* to be in the news. They want to be left alone to use their power, while the politicians distract us with their incessant electioneering. Don't we need newspeople to keep an eye on the bureaucrats who make up the "permanent government"? Yes, but they're not doing it. They never will. Reports of bureaucratic skullduggery or ineptitude can only be written after patient investigation, and they have to appear in sizeable studies, not in daily bits.

Now even if you accept everything I've said so far, you might still argue that because governments have become so incredibly powerful, we need an aggressive press to keep them in line. The most common example used is that of Senator Joseph McCarthy and his anticommunist crusade in the 1950s. The standard view is that journalist Edward R. Murrow of CBS news stood up to McCarthy at the risk of his career and began the senator's slide into oblivion.

But where did McCarthy's power come from? Obviously, from the news. The news follows anything that moves, and McCarthy was very skilled in keeping the cameras on himself. It has been said that he built his whole career on pseudo-events, trumpeted by reporters who couldn't stand the man. Richard Rovere, a reporter in Washington during McCarthy's heyday, recalled that

he knew how to get into the news even on those rare occasions when invention failed him and he had no unfacts to give out. For example, he invented the morning press conference called for the purpose of announcing an afternoon press conference. The reporters would come in—they were beginning, in this period, to respond to his summonses like Pavlov's dogs at the clang of a bell—and McCarthy would say that he just wanted to give them the word that he expected to be ready with a shattering announcement later in the day, for use in the papers the following morning. This would gain him a headline in the afternoon papers: "New McCarthy Revelations Awaited in Capital." Afternoon would come, and if McCarthy had some-thing, he would give it out, but often enough he had nothing, and this was a matter of slight concern. He would simply say that he wasn't quite ready, that he was having difficulty in getting some of the "documents" he needed or that a "witness" was proving elusive. Morning headlines: "Delay Seen in New McCarthy Case—Mystery Witness Being Sought."[5]

Daniel Boorstin also comments on McCarthy:

He had a diabolical fascination and an almost hypnotic power over news-hungry reporters. They were somehow reluctantly grateful to him for turning out their product. They stood astonished that he could make so much news from such meager raw material. Many hated him; all helped him. They were victims of what one of them called their "indiscriminate objectivity." In other words, McCarthy and the newsmen both thrived on the same synthetic commodity.

Senator McCarthy's political fortunes were promoted almost as much by newsmen who considered themselves his enemies as by those few who were his friends. Without the active help of all of them he could never have created the pseudo-events which brought him notoriety and power. Newspaper editors, who self-righteously attacked . . . him on the editorial page inside, were building him up in front-page headlines. . . . Honest newsmen and the unscrupulous Senator McCarthy were in separate branches of the same business.[6]

All of this was not because of bias or irresponsibility or incompetence of reporters; it was due to the periodical scheduling of our news.

Before we leave this episode, it is also worth noting that Murrow lost his job shortly after opposing McCarthy. CBS president William Paley decided that opposing McCarthy was too risky for a big corporation with a lot to lose.[7] Self-preservation is the first law of any institution like the news industry.

Of course we would all agree that politicians cannot be trusted with power. Power must be checked by power. The tragedy is that the press doesn't really use its power—its ability to get us all upset and angry—against government per se. Instead it is always helping to build up the power of the state. That may sound like a dubious proposition. Isn't the news usually attacking the government? Isn't this adversarial obsession what right-wing critics complain of? But consider what the press objects to. Isn't it usually that the state is being obstructed in some good purpose? The government is never doing *enough* to satisfy the press.

At one time newspapers may have challenged the establishment, but things have changed. Nowadays the news is a very large part of the establishment. It was back in 1828 that Thomas Macaulay called the reporters in the British Parliament chamber the "fourth estate of the realm."[8] Today one would be tempted to think of reporters as the first branch of government. Through their insistence they set our agenda as much as presidents do.

The Media Censor Our News

There is also the little-recognized fact that the news industry is the main censor today, rather than the government or the churches. That is, the media decide what we shouldn't hear in a kind of precensorship. What librarians or moral vigilantes do isn't censorship; they only want to keep libraries and schools from providing the books at taxpayer expense. They can't strangle ideas at their birth, like the news business can, simply by ignoring it. As A. J. Liebling put it, "Freedom of the press is guaranteed only to those who own one."[9]

The press's power to censor all expression is not due to its periodical character. It is due to the public's laziness; we take in only what we can get in periodical form—in small, predigested, daily bites. There are plenty of books out there that would enlighten us, but we are satisfied to read only the reviews by journalists who may be more interested in seeing the ideas dismissed. Can you imagine what a review of this book would look like?

But although the news ignores many ideas, it badgers legislators to produce initiatives that can be processed as news. Politicians are happy to oblige because news is advertising for them and everything they want to do. It gives incumbents their advantage in elections. So if the press were to disappear, government would not necessarily grow to fill the vacuum that was left. Government would diminish, incumbency would lose its advantage, and we would miss the advertisements for government programs. Washington insiders affirm what we have all suspected: our politicians' most prevalent motive is to be noticed and applauded.[10] It follows that if busy politicians didn't get noticed, there would be far less busyness. All the fun would go out of politics. Or at least all the fun politicians would go out of politics.

Politicians understand their dependence on the news. In France, Italy, Sweden and Norway, at least, they have reacted to the decline of news consumption in a very characteristic way—by giving government subsidies to the press.[11] Our Congress has also begun talking about requiring the media to give a certain minimum of attention to their campaigns, as we shall see.

Even communist states understood the relation of politics and the press. They all had news media. Their news, like ours, didn't have to be honest or free to build up the state's image and power. It only had to be daily. Of course in those countries the state really was the whole story, so their news was a better reflection of reality than ours is—yet. But like here, news was a main prop of the regime. The daily barrage of coverage given to political institutions focused attention on the state, just like it does here.

News and political power feed on each other. It has been so from the beginning. In England's history, for example, newspapers made their breakthrough in the immediate aftermath of the revolution of 1688—precisely when party politics began. The news industry was established to follow political activities and ended up prodding them along. Often the politicians financed their own papers, but it wasn't necessary; commercial considerations were sufficient to direct a periodical press toward a politics of incessant movement.

Don't go away—we have an election report coming up next!

PROVING THAT NEWS SPEEDS UP POLITICS

• *Boston Globe,* May 22, 1989: "No Improvement Cited in Marcos' Condition"

•   *Boston Herald,* same day: "Marcos Shows Improvement"

•   *Los Angeles Times,* June 3, 1989: "Parties Seeking to Curb Partisan Ethics Warfare"

• Same paper, same day: "Republicans Create Unit to Dig Up Any Damaging Data on Democrats"

5

Politics as a Perpetual Campaign

----

lmost everyone is dismayed by the quality of American political campaigns and their lack of substance. The key to understanding this situation is recognizing the dailiness of those campaigns and the related fact that electioneering doesn't stop with elections anymore. Politics has become a perpetual campaign. The point of this, of course, is so the networks can sell more advertising time for mouthwash and toilet-bowl cleaner. But the country pays a high price for them. For if our news-driven politics doesn't drive good candidates away from politics altogether, it is likely to trip them up on the way to a nomination or destroy their effectiveness in office.

Nothing is easier for the news to cover than a political campaign. Reporters know exactly where the news will happen, they know when the climax is due, and they know that their customers think it is all-important. For over a year there will be something on our presidential campaigns in each day's news. There are democracies in the world that don't allow their elections to go on like this. Their political elites—the people who have to submit to the indignities of electioneering—have not let things get out of control to this extent. But I hope they are listening, because they need to know where the dynamics of daily publication will drive them. We can see a later stage of these developments in this country, and it isn't a sight for the squeamish.

The news doesn't touch heavily on candidates' views on issues or their general philosophies. Politicians will allude to a number of crises that need to be addressed, of course. But the newspeople aren't interested in long discussion, because they sense that *we* aren't interested. What are we interested in, if not in debate on the characteristics of a good society? Basically the media think we are interested in "momentum." This is in line with the notion that a new reality is out there every day. We get daily reports on who has this momentum. Woe betide the candidate who has "sparked little excitement" recently. It won't matter where he or she stands on the issues if the country is not "responding." Such a candidate would never be able to offer the necessary leadership.

Thus political life begins to imitate soap opera: What gaff did candidate X make today? Did candidate Y offend candidate Z with the negative ad she ran? Did she apologize? Did he accept the apology? Did he do so with any grace? Will he retaliate? Have we heard the last of this episode? This drama is more diverting than politics, which is concerned with the use of power, the allocation of resources, setting priorities, strategic planning. Of course the news industry never said it would tell us how to make a wise choice in any of these matters. It just promised to tell the story of the campaign—a continuing story, perfect for selling tomorrow's advertising space. Extended discourse is the job of books —if anyone still reads books.

The news industry is not a public-service charity; it needs to turn a profit. So newspeople focus on momentum and blame the voters for not focusing on the issues. If we need to fix blame, it should be on our appetite for daily news. Someone has the figures to show that the average sound bite has fallen from 42.3 seconds to 9.8 in the last twenty years. This is our attention span for the issues. In elitist Britain, where campaigns are only three weeks long, TV might give candidates five whole minutes to offer their views. If those five minutes are boring, it is the candidate's problem, not the network's. In other words, the British media have not yet learned that politics can be part of the entertainment business.

Our American politicians have learned this, however. They understand that the management of the campaign is more important than its "substance." We enjoy the cut and thrust of a campaign more than the hard choices of policy debate. The media give us what we seem to want. In the election of 1968, 6 percent of all campaign stories were about "campaign theater." In 1988 over half (52 percent) were![1] Newspeople profess to dislike the antics the politicians use to get their attention, and they will sometimes take time to expose the politicians' use of manipulation—which means even less time for us to learn about the issues.

So we have campaigns in which the most indelible memory is of a candidate saying, "Where's the beef?" over and over. It got a lot of attention at the time. It was important because it related to real life—that is, to a TV commercial. (For those of you who don't remember, this was Walter Mondale's most memorable statement of 1984, echoing a hamburger commercial.) We still imagine that the campaign is supposed to be about something else. But if campaign theater is what sells papers, then it *is* the news. (Remember our definition.) And if getting elected is what politics is all about, these tricks *are* our politics.

When you think about it, maybe this concentration on image management and momentum *is* the best way to elect our president. What is a president but the person who will manage our news for the next four years? Whoever can handle the news better must be the better choice. It's something to think about, anyway.

What kind of politician does this style of campaigning produce? Do we get better presidents as campaign news coverage lasts longer? (You are shaking your head.) Doesn't our country produce people more capable than these candidates are? Why don't they run for office? Well, would you want to be president if you knew it would mean living in the news spotlight? The most capable people don't run because they are already complete people; they don't need to be news. It's not just the baddies who want to hide from its glare.

The Daily Referendum

Which brings us to the real topic of this chapter—the fact that the campaign doesn't end with the election any more. The end of the election is only the signal to begin another phase, which is the daily referendum on the country's choice. How does he or she stand in the polls? What is today's approval rating? Editors are particularly dogged about this phase if the country's choice wasn't their choice. The implied question in a thousand stories is, Are we sure we chose the right person? Does this administration have any legitimacy any longer? Remember, there are a lot more papers to sell.

Sometimes for weeks on end everything in the news is related to "the president's popularity." Politicians put up with this permanent campaign because they want to be reelected. The news gives them a considerable advantage in that they can start the next election campaign the minute the previous election is over. They know the newspeople need stories, so they will create them. We hear the winning stories on the evening news.

Hedrick Smith, in *The Power Game: How Washington Works*, describes how successive presidents have gone further and further toward tailoring their policies to daily reporting. There was a rule in Nixon's administration that any official who wanted to put a public event on the president's schedule had to have a good idea of what the headline would be, what the picture accompanying the story would show and what the lead paragraph would say. Michael Deaver jetted President Reagan all over America to photograph him in front of schools, housing projects and forests in an effort to shape the public's view of him—without, of course, changing Reagan's policies in the least.[2] If we got our political news on a monthly basis—say, in extended treatments—this sort of activity would lose its whole point.

You might think there is nothing wrong in watching the polls if it only shows a deference to public opinion. This is a democracy, after all. But it is one thing to be concerned about what voters will think by the next election; it is quite another thing to worry about *each day's* ratings in the endless referendum that the news sponsors. A government's fear of offending anybody, anywhere, anytime, even for one week destroys all continuity in policy.

Nothing drives home the point that government is the proper focus of all serious attention like this perpetual political campaign does. We almost imagine that government could correct the lack of love in our families, the lack of respect among the races, the lack of responsibility between classes, the violence of our entertainment and its spinoff into our lives, the boredom that leads to drugs or the decadence of our arts. How have we come to think of government as the solution for such problems?

The attempt to politicize all problems—a natural consequence of daily news—is one of the dumbest aspects of modern life. Daniel Bell remarked that one of the dopey things about the liberal tradition (shared by both parties in our broadly "liberal" society) is that it turns life's existential questions into "problems." Given our dynamic view of politics, we tend to assume that where there is a problem there must be a "solution," meaning a political solution.[3] If we thought about it, we could probably agree that the solutions to our deepest problems lie in attitudes, not in power or money.

What is usually needed is hope and love and personal goals. But if a politician made this point, he or she would be accused of being irresponsible. He or she wouldn't fit the news paradigm of a serious politician.

Missing the Real Issues

When newspeople do take up a momentous issue, like education, they are apt to make a hash of it. I used to watch for articles on education in the local paper when my kids were in school. There was almost nothing. If the school had a program on "AIDS education," that would be featured. When children were gunned down in a schoolyard half a continent away, we would get an exposé of the lack of security around our local schools. But there was almost nothing on student accomplishment or teacher effort.

Every other year there was a school-board election that always got a lot of ink. But in the absence of earlier discussion, we were not sure whether the candidates had focused on the real problems. Only the elections were news. They could be personalized, and they sold a month's worth of papers. But after that, again, nothing. We never heard what the winning candidates did unless they were caught having an affair with a principal.

Education is a process that reveals deeply held values and concerns. But education is not a crisis or a tragedy or even an event. As a result, we are tempted to think that it can't be as important as the things on the front page. That is the way our news-obsessed minds work. When the media can politicize it, we feel it is becoming important. The standard way they do this is to report the spending figures announced by government agencies (which means we'll never hear about private or parochial education). Unfortunately, the federal allocation—decided by the heavy hitters in the news world—is a tiny fraction of the money supporting education, and little of it goes to the classroom.

As far as educational performance goes, it is widely recognized that the quality of family life is more important than anything that goes on in school. The news even reported studies that revealed this fact. But no one seriously thinks that government can change our families or create a positive attitude toward the culture our schools try to teach about.

Editors invariably fail to draw the logical conclusion to this dilemma. In their world, when there is a problem there should be something the government can do about it. Otherwise we'd all be on our own. So they talk about money. And they make education part of the permanent campaign, the daily referendum on our leaders. Headlines shame our governors with the news of another "cut" in educational funds. Maybe the governors should be ashamed, maybe not. Maybe they know of the waste involved in efforts to look innovative or busy. Maybe they know they can't help students who no longer have any curiosity or who imagine that anything they need to know will be on the news. The governors won't get any such message out through the press. Newspeople are reluctant to suggest that the problem might be in ourselves—their customers.

We can't debate issues when they are reduced to bumper-sticker proportions. We can't take time to consider situations when our focus changes daily. There isn't room in the paper for the insights of those with the largest views, nor is our attention span what it once was. Instead we will be kept abreast of the politics of the issue, who has the votes or by what trickery the minority might get its way. For example, one study of the recent "debate" on health care showed that 35 percent of news coverage was devoted to discussion of the issues involved, whereas 54 percent was given to political strategy.[4]

Again, this is nobody's fault. It is just a function of how the issues confronting us are marketed in our system. The question whether there is a better way to do these things will have to await a later chapter. So don't touch that dial!

A BUSY DAY ON THE EDUCATION FRONT

- *Wall Street Journal,* September 12, 1989: "Scores on College Entrance Tests Fall"
- *USA Today,* same day: "SAT Scores End '80s Up"
- *New York Times,* same day: "Minority Students Gain on College Entrance Tests"
- *Westchester-Rockland Daily News,* same day: "SAT Scores Take Dip for Women, Minorities"

Or none of the above?

6

Why
News Product
Looks Nothing
like History

Phil Graham, onetime owner of the *Washington Post,* used
to say that news is the first draft of history. He meant that
journalists do the hard work and scholars tie up the loose
ends for the more permanent record. Would that it were so simple.
Actually, even those who have read the news for years will not be
prepared for the story that historians will eventually tell.

Take another example. Back on April 6, 1987, *Time* magazine
breathlessly reported ("it's a biggie," they said) a scandal involving
Marine guards at the American embassy in cold-war Moscow. It
appeared that some of them had been fraternizing with attractive
enemy agents and selling U.S. secrets. The government had initi-
ated court-martial proceedings against a Native American and an
African American. Two weeks later the matter was given four
stories in another issue of *Time.*

A few months later (July 20), however, *Time* decided that it had
been misled. The magazine printed a picture of one of the accused

with the caption "Bracy, vindicated, in New York last week." The story told us that "no Soviet bug has yet been found anywhere in the current embassy." It seemed that the whole affair was the result of "aggressive, overzealous agents of the Naval Investigative Service." Reporters got an unnamed diplomat to say that "there are forces of darkness, if you want to call them that, who oppose any kind of long-term improvement in U.S.-Soviet relations." Beyond that, "a Marine general in Washington with detailed knowledge of the case" admitted that this was not a major espionage case.

By November 23 *Time* wanted to pursue the matter further, having decided that the government was trying to cover up its handling of the victims of this hoax. The magazine suggested that "somebody ought to be investigating the investigators." That would make a good story, of the long, drawn-out variety. And it would have the usual villains—military people and racial bigots.

On February 20, 1989, *Time* got another cover story out of this episode. Another bombshell, in fact. It then appeared that the espionage had been "far worse than anyone feared—or the Government will admit." Another embarrassment for the government. Another coup for the investigative press. Actually, *Time* was encouraged to reopen the case by a book on the subject, Ronald Kessler's *Moscow Station: How the KGB Penetrated the American Embassy.* But "in a cover story and numerous articles, *Time* made a similar assessment," they boasted. Ahead of the historians.

In this new version of the story *Time* seemed to be ahead of the government, which was accused of having tried to suppress it from the first. (Mind you, this is the same government that had filed the charges that tipped *Time* off to the story.) The magazine blamed government suppression for the fact that "the spy furor quickly faded away." In fact, furor fades away when editors get tired of it.

But wait, there's more. In its July 10, 1989, issue *Time* had to

Of course we all recognize that the news is there to give some excitement to our humdrum lives, but still, we want to think that our information has *some* permanent validity. To be sure, some of the newsmagazine's articles will still be of value—the ones that comment on more general trends. They will be buried deep inside the magazine, though, because they are not news. The hard news will suffer the most from the passage of just a few weeks.

Take for example the hard news from the summer of 1985. That was not considered to be a slow news summer. In fact, William Safire, a columnist who tries to provide some sort of historical perspective, complained in his column on September 20, 1985, that things were happening too quickly for the news to deal adequately with events. What were these events that were pursued for several months with the usual end-of-the-world headlines? There was the search for an ex-Nazi named Josef Mengele who, it was thought, might still be alive. There was the uproar over President Reagan's plan to visit Bitburg cemetery in Germany, which turned out to contain graves of Nazis. There was the seizure of an airliner by some Muslim terrorists, which captured us all for three weeks. The South African government made news by trying to censor *Newsweek*'s reporting. And the president had his colon-cancer crisis, which might easily have turned into a tragedy.

It is conceivable that some of these events will be included in a history of our time. If so, they will be in a form that is not apparent yet. But it all worked just fine as news; it kept us tuned in. Isn't it a little embarrassing to think that we were all agog over such stuff? Don't you wonder what was going on that summer that *will* be part of history?

Essentially, the reason that old papers and magazines seem quaint and naive is that newspeople can't keep from leaning over into the future. We have made them the prophets of our secular age. Prophets, you remember, were those who gave God's perspective on events. That's why they might know what was going to happen next as well as what was really significant about the past. Prophets placed events in the perspective of the whole of history. This is precisely what the news cannot do with its lack of a time dimension.

The results of this prophetic pretense are often embarrassing. Take the stories on the 1990 Oakland Athletics baseball team at playoff time. The team was so awesome that *Time* (October 8, 1990) declared that "the A's know that their true opponents will not be the Pirates or Red Sox or Reds, but the ghosts of great teams past." The Reds were less impressed and went on to sweep the A's in the World Series. In sports it is pretty obvious when newspeople don't know the score. On other subjects it is harder for us to keep track of their record.

Now you might object, "So what if news doesn't have any eternal significance? Life is in flux. News is like breathing. If you want to get philosophical about things, you can do that when you're old and out of it." I have nothing against breathing, though there isn't anything very interesting to say about it. But our lives—both our individual and our societal lives—are more like stories; they have a beginning, middle and end. To be satisfying or instructive, a biography has to cover a person's whole life. Events enter real history when we can close the book on them. Only then will we have learned something about being human.

Not everyone knows that history is supposed to teach us what it is to be human and what humans have proved capable of. There are a lot of wrestling coaches teaching history who present it as just a bunch of things in the past. That is what news is, after all. Maybe they got their idea of history from the news.

Facts and Truth

Back in the seventeenth century, when the news industry began, a cult of "the facts" came into existence. This concentration on facts was a liberating reaction against a preachy culture that always told people what to think about things. The news wanted to be neutral and transparent, to simply deal in the events themselves and not in the moral of the story. So it borrowed the concept of the isolated "fact" from the law courts, giving each event a recognized source, a specific location in time and space, and some kind of closure.[1] The concept of *fact* has gone on to have a celebrated career in science, but only when such facts are brought together into larger patterns. Because of its periodical nature, news must disconnect facts in order to hype each day's edition. News stories are like mysteries in which some facts serve *to keep us in the dark* until the story reaches a final resolution that hardly interests us. We see this today in our long-running "investigations."

We've already mentioned the attention paid to airline crashes. I could understand noting them somewhere near the obituary section. But why make them lead stories in the world news? What is the significance of an airline crash? What is the significance of two airline crashes, for that matter? Many more people die in car crashes around the world on any given day than die in a single plane crash. Those deaths *are* part of a pattern, but that pattern doesn't make the news. And yet people will stop flying after reading about a plane crash and pile into their cars instead. This is what news does to our thinking.

You might also say that things become news precisely because we *don't* understand them. If they are seen to be part of a historical pattern, they aren't surprising or newsworthy. News covers the odd and the out-of-the-way. It is a distraction from rather than a first draft of history. That would be all right if news were just a small part of the information we take in. But if it *is* our information intake, we begin to lose our way.

What Makes Something Historic?
From time to time the news announces some upcoming event as "historic" to make sure we are tuned in when it happens. It is

interesting to see what their idea of historic is. Often it is a meeting of heads of state who will put their signatures on some document. Newspeople remember that there are many such events in the history books, so they think this too must be history. What they forget is that most such meetings and documents did *not* get into the history books, because they didn't turn out to be significant in the long term. We simply cannot know which historical turning points are passing right under our noses, but they are unlikely to be the queen of England's visit with the premier of China or the dedication of a new spaceport. The presence of scores of heads of state (and hundreds of journalists) does not necessarily make something "historic" in the sense of explaining how we got where we are now.

Recently a former managing editor of the *New York Times* made a list of the ten biggest stories—or most historic events—of the twentieth century. Five of the ten items had to do with the two world wars, which is understandable. He also included the Bolshevik and Roosevelt revolutions, along with the Wright brothers' first flight, the creation of the atom bomb and the landing on the moon.

Otto Friedrich, who is a more reflective journalist than most, pointed out that penicillin and pesticides have saved more lives than were lost in the wars, that television and birth control have altered our society and values beyond all recognition, that computers have transformed business and that nothing was said of any cultural milestones. In other words, the editor's list is what one would expect from a journalist. He was most impressed with the destructive forces of our times. But, as Friedrich asks, who remembers who was president when F. Scott Fitzgerald wrote his novels? "What does anyone know about the petty princelings who ruled Germany in the time of Bach except that they were not very kind to Bach? What does anyone know about the Pope who built the Sistine Chapel except that he hired Michelangelo to paint the ceiling?"[2] If you tried to write the history of the Renaissance from the news of that day, you would miss everything that we treasure from that time.

In 1991 *Time* made Ted Turner its Man of the Year because he "made history" in a whole new sense, giving us "History As It Happens," in their words. Actually the history of 1991—its meaning in a larger sense—won't be written in our lifetime. When I tell my students that, they protest, "Well how *can* we know what is really going on now, if not from the news?" The answer is, we can't. Historians are no wiser than the rest of us about the meaning of today. Ted Turner and his industry peers will not write the history of our time. But they will be part of that history, of the increasing trend to overemphasize news.

Revising History

The news does just as bad a job of revising the historical record as they do of creating it. On September 14, 1990, my local paper headlined the finding that Mozart died of kidney failure, which supposedly upset earlier theories. Anyone interested in Mozart had always known that he died of kidney failure; it is stated in every musty old dictionary of music. But reporters don't consult old dictionaries. They hype the latest "interpretations." Then they may get to rush to the rescue with even later studies. The very same paper announced an Egyptian scholar's theory that Moses was actually Pharaoh Akhenaton (or vice versa). I await new headlines concerning studies that will show that Moses was *not* actually Akhenaton "as is commonly believed." Nothing will ever be settled so long as there is another edition to sell. And sadly, historians will begin their investigations with visions of the headlines that will make them famous for their "new findings."

We had another instance of newspeople revising history on the first anniversary of Desert Storm, the 1991 United Nations military action against Iraq. Dan Rather, Peter Jennings, CNN, *Newsweek* and the *New York Times* all agreed that nothing had changed over there since

Desert Storm. That is to say, Saddam Hussein was still leader of Iraq.[3]

Actually nothing is really the same over there: Kuwait is different, Iraq is different, Hussein is different, Hussein's weapons program is different, we are different, the U.S. military is different. Whole books will be written on those differences someday. But news consumers only want a minute or two on the subject, and the most obvious thing to say was that the early expectations in that conflict were not realized. Who had created these expectations—that Saudi Arabia and Kuwait would become democracies and that a new order of peace would settle on the area? The news of course. The media cannot resist creating expectations because they will want to sell another edition tomorrow.

There is another, more mundane reason that history will elude the news, which we have already mentioned. That is the fact that powerful people—those who are making things happen—don't like to be in the news. This hardly needs proving. Watch the politicians and tycoons squirm when journalists put them on the spot.

Power is the ability to make people do what they don't want to do. Those who exercise power aren't keen on our knowing what's happening to us. They are glad when we chase celebrities instead. The best-laid plans never come to light. Once in a while investigative reporters do uncover the powers behind the scenes, and we should be thankful for that. But it is not necessary to make such revelations in the context of daily news reporting. In fact, it usually appears in books instead, in a much more coherent form.

The corollary of this axiom—power shuns publicity—is that if you only know what is in the newspapers, you are an outsider. It is odd how people preen themselves on knowing what the newspapers are saying. They mistakenly think that means they are "in the know." Actually it means just the opposite. People who are in the know watch news reports only to see what sense the reporters are making of things and what the "peasants" will soon be thinking.

Required Falsification

I have said that I will not name any villains in this book, but recounting deliberate falsification of history comes very close to such an accusation. Sometimes falsification is almost required in the interests of daily news. That is, journalists must sometimes alter their reports because of the requirements of periodical publication. There is a notable example of this in the total nonreporting of one of the biggest events of our century.

In the early 1930s, after the collectivization of agriculture in the Soviet Union, Joseph Stalin decided to reduce the population of the Ukraine by starvation. It was our first modern example of genocide, taking something between seven and fifteen million lives. The event has been reconstructed by a team of historians at Harvard who took special pains to be accurate because it seemed to be a sensitive subject.

Why was it sensitive? While it was going on, the *New York Times* correspondent in Moscow, Walter Duranty, denied the existence of any such famine. He knew better, but he also knew that if he reported it he would cease to be welcome in Stalin's capital. His daily news from Russia would cease. Apparently it wasn't as important that the news should be accurate as that there should *be* some news. Duranty got the Order of Lenin for his discretion. He also got the Pulitzer Prize in correspondence in 1932 for his coverage of Russia.

Fifty years later, in 1985, a documentary based on the Harvard historians' efforts was finally ready, and it won numerous international film awards. But to the producer's astonishment the media did not want to talk about it. PBS complained that the film presented only one point of view. That had not stopped them from showing documentaries on the Holocaust—a similar sort of cataclysm. *Time* did not want to discuss the incident because it was no longer news, although the magazine admitted that "we do occasionally report historical events when they bear directly on current news." In other words, *Time* saw no connection between this episode and the Balkanization that would help destroy the Soviet Union or the genocidal policies of several of its satellites. PBS's New York affiliate, WNET-TV, likewise refused to air the documentary because it did not present "the other side." It did not occur to them that this *was* the other side to the big lie that had been spread by the news.

Why all this self-censorship? *New York Times* critic Vincent Canby was finally candid enough to give an answer (October 10, 1985). Canby did not deny that Duranty had lied. Rather, he blamed the historians for not saying why he lied. And why had he lied? Because he had a job to do—writing news—and he couldn't do that if he told the truth.[4]

Think about that. Apparently Canby thinks he has answered the press's critics by saying that Duranty's dishonesty had nothing to do with leftist ideology. Duranty wasn't a "pinko" or something; he was a newsman, and he had to play the game by the rules. I guess that means he'd have lied for Adolf Hitler just as readily as he did for Stalin. Is that reassuring? You probably thought that the news existed to keep you informed. Actually it's just to keep you reading.

Take a more recent example. You may remember a bunch of stories in 1987-1988 about something called the "October Surprise." We read that there were some shady dealings between the Reagan people and the Iranian government even before Reagan was elected in 1980 that got Iran to delay the release of the U.S. embassy hostages until after President Carter had been defeated. The strung-out story grew and grew, as the media's secret witnesses' memories improved. It included reports of Palestine Liberation Organization training camps in Oregon, Israelis' training Columbian drug-cartel hit squads and the United States' selling weapons for drugs to bring home to the American market. The CIA's denial of the story became something like evidence of its truth, which is how witch-hunts work. One of those who "came forward" had a master's degree in "parapsychology" and disclosed, among other things, that U.S. satellites parted the clouds during Reagan's inaugural so that the sun would shine only on him.[5]

You might think that at this point reporters would have put away their pens. Instead they apparently thought, *What if this dingbat is mostly* right *and somebody else breaks this story? A lot of things that sound crazy turn out to be important.* Reporters can't judge— nobody could at that point. So they printed it. History would have its say, someday. Incidentally, this isn't the *National Enquirer* we're talking about but ABC, PBS, *Nation, Newsweek,* the *New York Times,* the *Los Angeles Times* and the *Miami Herald.*

When history did have its say, it wasn't on the front page, where the craziness had been. Do you remember any retractions when all the "witnesses" were discredited and the story dissolved? Probably not, and as a result you may have a little gritty residue in your mind from this episode, which is not connected to anything real. You're supposed to get history's judgment somewhere else.

We won't end on that sad note. Let's look at Walter Lippmann, a man the news industry is proud of, almost its patron saint. Writing in the 1930s and later, he was one of the first journalists who tried to create a context big enough for reporting on Congress, the nation, even the world. He did not get bogged down in the minutia of politics—the rumors and factional fighting—as did his peers. He wanted to keep his readers from being surprised at the events of the day, despite the difficulty of those times. In short, he tried to be a historian.

He can hardly be considered a journalist. As confirmation of that point, David Halberstam notes that while "other journalists were prisoners of events, tearing up long-planned vacations at the last minute" in order to cover some new U.S.-U.S.S.R. crisis, "Lippmann never did. At the beginning of the year he knew his entire schedule" for that year.[6] His career alternative was to have taught philosophy at Harvard. And some of his stuff is still worth reading.

FOR THOSE OF YOU WHO THINK IT'S ONLY THE HEADLINE WRITERS WHO GET CONFUSED

- *International Herald Tribune,* **January 21, 1989:**
  After an initial burst of anxiety immediately after his election, the financial markets have greeted the ascendancy of George Bush to the White House with a joy bordering on euphoria.

- **Same paper, same day,** *same page:*
  Currency markets and Wall Street showed little reaction to George Bush's swearing-in as president and currency dealers said his inaugural address had been mainly neutral for the dollar.

  Which was the first draft of history?

7

How News Turns Science into Superstition

You might think that if news has as little sympathy for religion as I have indicated, then it might be fairly encouraging to science. We would be hard-pressed to remember any slighting comments newspeople have made about science per se. But actually what news does to real science is as destructive as what it does to religion.

Remember our theme: having to sell a paper every day or a magazine every week requires that the news industry treats every interim report as if it were real knowledge, worthy of our full attention. In other words, news must treat each discovery as if it were in some way final. Think how the "results" of science appear in your paper. We see more and more about nutrition, for example. "Studies show" that decaffeinated coffee is "bad for you." We heard it on the news, we say. But is that actually what the scientists said?

Maybe you've never read a scientific paper. Reading them can be a letdown for those of us who have been overstimulated by news reports. Take a journal report in psychology, for instance. It will tell us that a study was conducted using thirty-seven freshman psychology students at the University of Wisconsin (really some teaching assistant's discussion section). This study used the XYZ Attitude Survey, which differentiates liberal and conservative leanings, in order to show possible correlation with those same students' self-report of certain activities. A correlation of, say, .123 proved "significant" at the .12 level of probability, which prompted some scientific journal to print it, in order to stimulate further research. But the headline reads: "Study Links Conservatism and Bed-Wetting." There is no fine print, only the usual slashing style of the journalist. "Reasons" are advanced as to the cause of this interesting "link."

These days we are getting wary of such reports. For one thing, we are aware of the rapid changes in the diets suggested by nutritional reports. We remember the frequent scares over eating certain foods that that were reversed later. But when the news reverses itself and reports the "all clear," we believe that too. We believe anything we are told that scientists believe. The trouble is that scientists don't "believe in" the results of their efforts in the same way that the news does. For newspeople, science is a new belief system. And it has the advantage—unlike other belief systems—of changing pretty frequently.

There aren't any factual discoveries in philosophy or religion. Philosophical and religious developments come primarily through the broadening of perspectives and refinements in expression. But science is something one needs to keep abreast of, and the periodical press offers to help us do that. Actual scientists must wince when they see how their work is reported in the media. For they don't think of their studies as final. They recognize the disappointingly small scale of their interim discoveries and know how many studies are needed before one can make a simple—that is, a general—statement.

Newspeople rush in where scientists fear to tread. We had a taste of this at the beginning of the reporting on AIDS. Editors didn't want us to be unduly alarmed—just alarmed enough to buy tomorrow's report. It seemed that AIDS was very easy to catch or very hard to catch, depending on the story. If they were emphasizing the epidemic crisis and addressing potential victims, AIDS was easy to catch. If they were addressing the rest of us and emphasizing the lack of humaneness shown by nurses or schoolteachers, then it was almost impossible to catch, if all went well.

Newswriters couldn't decide whether to terrorize us with talk of an epidemic or shame us for shunning those who were infected. So they did both. Nothing was more common than for them to tell us all the ways that one could not get AIDS—say, from mosquito bites. But no scientist had concluded that. The most that a scientist could say was that no case had yet been reported that could only have resulted from such a bite. In other words, a case might have been caused by a mosquito, but because the subject also was exposed by another factor—which was known to be the cause in other cases— the bite seemed redundant and unlikely. But if the scientists were not altogether definite, the newspeople were.

What does all this have to do with periodicity? The news wants to report the future of science. It is typical high-risk journalism, reporting from the "leading edge." So the science that is newsworthy is the science that is still half-baked. And if our memories were not so enfeebled by periodicity, we could all remember when "science" had changed its mind.

I remember several news reports from the winter of 1988 that cast doubt on the idea that alcoholism is a "disease." This disease theory had been the orthodoxy of several generations, as the news had helped to create greater sympathy for alcoholics. I suppose there had always been "experts" who had doubted that the metaphor of *disease* was really appropriate to this complicated issue.

But if there were, they weren't the experts that the news cited. (Have you ever noticed how even the experts don't get to complete their sentences in news reports? Like others, they are cut off as soon as they've said what the news wants us to hear.)

Anyway, suddenly this view—that alcohol addiction involved a "character disorder" if not moral failure, not a disease—was getting a hearing. For decades it had only been expressed by spokespersons for the Woman's Christian Temperance Union, who were exhibited as examples of what scientific enlightenment was up against.

So what was happening? Had experts changed their minds? Actually, what had happened is that one of President Reagan's cronies (remember Michael Deaver?) was using the addiction-as-a-disease defense in his influence-peddling trial, and newspeople weren't going to let him get away with it. So they turned to the other school of thought for its expertise. This theory was now news not because science had changed its collective mind, but because newspeople decided to give it a hearing. We should be prepared, however, for another reversal of all this some time down the line, when a new view will sell papers.

Who Are These Experts?
By the way, who are these experts? How do we know that they are really experts? I have some personal experience of being mistaken for an expert. Newspapers and radio stations sometimes call my department for academic expertise on a variety of subjects. This is doubtless a good thing for them to do. But our busy secretaries have been known to pass reporters along to any one of us, just to get rid of them. In half the cases they send to me I am not an expert, and sometimes I have only a bare knowledge of the subject. Think of the havoc I could wreak if I decided to string the reporters along. If they liked what they were hearing, their readers might be badly taken in, thinking they were getting expert opinion.

Sometimes the news wants to report on a very uncertain area in which experts differ more noticeably than usual. Editors or producers may bring in a couple of experts and let them "debate" the issue for us, which is perhaps as much as the media can do. But the forum (parallel columns in print or a whole ten minutes on TV) is rarely enlightening. We may like one expert better than the other for any one of a dozen reasons. Or we might never learn who was more truly "expert."[1]

The news can't judge expertise in most fields. On April 4, 1991, columnist Tom Wicker wanted to consider the climatic results of the Kuwaiti oil fires. "Some authorities predict a global warming effect. . . . Others foresee a sort of 'nuclear winter,' " he told us. "Other experts dispute such predictions." Now wait. Those are pretty big differences. If experts predict either a warming or a cooling trend or they deny the validity of predictions, what makes them experts? They must be experts on something else. Apparently Wicker decided it was better to offer speculation than to be silent. Publication schedules mean we've got to say something. News marches on, whether science does or not.

Of course experts can differ and still be "experts" in the sense of knowing much more than the rest of us. I'm just arguing that newspeople can't know who the experts are without being experts themselves. All experts are not equal, and it is unfortunate that editors make the final judgments between them so far as public perception is concerned.

Sometimes in its search for expertise the news gets so intrigued by really cooperative scientists that these people become news items in themselves. News likes to personalize its reports, and since science can be a little abstract, reporters will build up certain scientific celebrities. The trouble with scientific celebrity is that it tends to involve quirky ideas on other subjects. A gabby astronomer, for instance, might have "interesting" views on spirit travel. Which of the astronomer's comments do you think the news will begin to focus on?

You might think you have caught me in a contradiction here. I said that scientists must not like dealing with sensation-mongering reporters, and now I'm suggesting that they may like a little publicity. I still think the general principle holds. And I also suspect that there is a distinction to be made between those who work in the "hard sciences" like physics or genetics and those who work in the social sciences. I haven't done a study to prove it, but I sense that the temptation toward publicity is greater with sociologists and psychologists. Theirs is the kind of science that touches us most directly. We look to them for wisdom about life, and some of them do not seem to mind being called on to pronounce on our social issues.

Scientists who aspire to media celebrity know what is expected of them—they must be original. This results is a tendency toward mildly sensational "scientific" reports on societal issues. A few years ago the news was full of reports about the waning of the "traditional family." We were told repeatedly that only a dwindling fraction of American families were of the traditional kind—with a working father, an at-home mother and their children. It was no longer the "norm" in American life. So it seemed to follow that one shouldn't take that family pattern as an ideal any longer. Certainly one shouldn't look askance at other "models" of family relationships. After all, one of them might become the new norm. The journalists seemed to want to save readers from any guilt or shame for not conforming to an outdated pattern.

How would a real scientist view all this? Some of them noticed that the journalists' figures were simply mistaken. A director at the National Institute of Education had claimed that "in 1955, 60 percent of the households in the U.S. consisted of a working father, a housewife mother and two or more school-age children. . . . In

1985 it is 7 percent, an astonishing change." It turned out that he was wrong and the figure for 1955 was closer to 22 percent.[2] But in order to really understand these figures, one would also need to know how many families did not yet have two or more school-age children but would someday, how many families that fit the old pattern had children past school age, how many mothers or fathers worked part time in an effort to preserve part of the traditional pattern, how families with adopted or foster children were being counted and so on.

Scientists might also want to know how those parents felt about their situation, how hard they were trying to maintain some ideal pattern or how willing they were to change. This is part of the objective situation too. But one had the feeling that the news had an agenda in concentrating on changes. It is in the interests of the news industry to give us the feeling that change is coming fast. That will mean that we'll need more news than ever, since only the news can be our guide in a revolutionary environment.

News reports from the social sciences inevitably are disturbing to anyone who is comfortable with the present situation. That is the only reason for such reporting. There would be no point in confirming the conventional wisdom unless somehow this would be surprising. News is about surprises, and journalists are successful when they have convinced us that our world is about to be overwhelmed by change. It means we'll need to see their next program or read their next issue.

For example, if half of all marriages are "working," that would not be news; they are supposed to work. If half of all marriages aren't working, however, that is news. These are two ways of looking at the same situation! What it means is that a story like this one has to be reported in the latter way—to the disadvantage of custom. Even if only 10 percent of marriages didn't succeed, they would still be the newsworthy ones, rather than the 90 percent that were "supposed to" succeed.

Unsettling news of this sort will be repeated until we get the sense that marriage will soon be a thing of the past. This may become a self-fulfilling prophecy if the power of suggestion can change our behavior. It will certainly affect children who hear it often enough. Thus what purports to be social science becomes part of the media's self-serving campaign for change.

Norms Versus Ideals

Those who feel that the press is nagging them to change should remember that real science stops short of making choices for us. What I'm getting at is that we should make our choices according to our *ideals* rather than according to the statistical *norms* or averages that are so much easier for the news to report.

Ideals and norms are often confused in our society. An ideal is what you are trying to do, whereas a norm is what you are already doing. Or more accurately, the norm is the average behavior of the lot of us. Ideal behavior might not be reached by any of us but may still be very important. We could be tugged in the direction of the ideal even though we aren't there yet. Scientists can study ideals as well as norms. But the news doesn't seem as interested in ideals, and one can see why.

Reporters are mesmerized by trends and cannot help suggesting that we should be guided by the movement of norms. News has less to say about our ideals, because these are more resistant to change. You might be convinced that some present trend is destructive. You might think that some current norms can never prove to be a viable practice. A few good examples—or even an unreachable ideal— might be a more powerful force than the social trends that impress our journalists.

News has little to say about our ideals. They change too slowly to be part of the news. But norms do change, back and forth, which qualifies them as news. Stories speak of those who "cling to" unfashionable ideas or practices "in the face of recent trends" as if they are social fossils. Newspeople are not getting this from social scientists, who know that a norm is not a guide to life.

When we feel bad about trends, it means that our norms and ideals are pretty far apart. That is nothing new; it is part of being human. People have always had to struggle to reach their ideals, but we need not give them up just because we have not yet reached them. The news often seems to want to relieve us of guilt by showing that our ideals are not a universal reality. It is not doing us a favor in this, and it is not being scientific. Nor are legislators doing us a favor by thinking that they need to adjust the law to the norms they read about in the news.

What does periodicity have to do with all this? The media are not willing to leave any of us behind. They want their audience to move together into the future. The news is not going to admit that a large number of us do not intend to "move with the times." Yet without the news's prodding, people might simply remain divided on questions like family patterns. In short, you can choose whether you want to join in the trends that news promotes. But if you don't join in, you may not find your world represented in news discourse.

How News Drives Science

The news and politicians who follow it most closely have a marked impact on science as well as on our image of science. For example, legislators may direct government funding of medicine and social science toward trendy topics. Ambitious scientists know how to design studies that will play to these trends so as to ensure funding.

Perhaps the most notorious instance of how news can corrupt science was in the launch of the space shuttle *Challenger* in 1986. NASA was founded in part to create publicity for the government and to show our tax dollars at work. Congressional favor could have gone to a lot of other science projects that might have brought a greater return in human welfare or knowledge, but the results would not have been as newsworthy. So NASA was given a sixty-person staff to manage press coverage and to convince viewers (voters) of NASA's need for support. It was acutely embarrassed, therefore, at the repeated delays in the shuttle launches during the 1980s. If those officials had responded to actual scientific and technical concerns, they would have taken the time and the pains to do things right. Unfortunately they were tuned in to the news.

The *New York Times* called one of the delays in the *Challenger* launch a "comedy of errors," and the *Washington Post* began its story of the aborted launch on January 27 with a parody of "For the want of a nail the horse was lost." ABC's *World News Tonight* said sarcastically, "Once again a flawless liftoff proved to be too much of a challenge for the *Challenger.*" *CBS Evening News* seemed exasperated: "Yet another costly, red-faces-all-around space-shuttle-launch delay. This time a bad bolt on a hatch and a bad-weather bolt from the blue are being blamed. . . . Confidence in NASA's ability to maintain a launch schedule has been rocked by this series of embarrassing technical snafus and weather delays." A director at the Kennedy Manned Space Flight Center later said in an interview with the *Washington Post* that such news treatment created "98 percent of the pressure" to go ahead with the disastrous mission.[3] You may remember that the *Challenger* shuttle was carrying along a teacher to ensure news coverage. This is what happens when science gets too close to the news. Scientists manipulate the politicians through the news and its viewers. But their own research agendas get distorted, and they may pay a heavy price when their science is judged by a fickle public.

While awaiting actual discoveries NASA entertains us with speculation on whether the universe is going to collapse into a great heap or continue expanding infinitely. In 1992 the NASA public-relations staff claimed that data collected by the Hubble Telescope offered evidence for infinite expansion. Actually it only confirmed something scientists had known for fifteen years but which they did not think proved anything of the sort. But NASA treated it as a new discovery, since they needed some good news about Hubble. In 1993 there was another report, using data from an x-ray satellite, supposedly confirming the opposite—that there was enough "dark matter" and hence gravity to indicate that the universe would eventually constrict. Scientists, again, must grind their teeth when they see these conflicting headlines. But as one of them said, "How else can you get closing the universe to compete with Michael Jordan's sprained ankle?"[4]

As it is presented to us in news reports, science is little more than superstition. Readers see figures on social norms, for example, and assume that they are something one could find in nature. They are not; they are statistical abstractions. The *range* of responses or conditions is what is "real," not the norms. But that range is too complicated to report. Nor does the news tell us how limited the evidence was on which the scientific report is based. Correlations are understood as perfect rather than merely suggestive. Results are looked upon as conclusive rather than indicative. Whereas true science must always hold itself open to new evidence and new conceptualizations, news science must hype today's report as if it were definitive.

Knowing Everything

Behind the news hype is the illusion that all these sciences are just about complete and that we may soon know just about everything. As you've noticed, the anticipated "theory of everything" is finding its way into news reports, threatening to chase black holes off page one. It is never made clear that scientists do not even pretend that such a theory (accounting for basic forces) will actually *explain* everything.

Sad to say, we cannot know how close we are to "finishing" any of the sciences, whatever that would mean. Only when such a body of knowledge is "complete" would one know its full dimensions. Until that time, we cannot know whether we are about done or have only just begun. But the news gives us the impression that scientists are getting near to closure—real certainty—and are engaged in a mopping-up operation. For what would be the point of reporting scientific formulations that will prove to be initial instead of conclusive steps? If there still are scientists two hundred years from now, they may be showing how primitive our present notions are.

Scientists are in this for the long haul and will look puzzled if you ask them when their sciences will be finished. Social scientists are in an even worse situation, since they are tracking a moving target; the answers to their questions about society will have to be different one hundred years from now, when societies are different. Yet the news won't grab us if it doesn't treat scientific reports with an air of conclusiveness and closure.

It's odd when you think about it. It would seem natural for periodicals to give the opposite impression—that science is in considerable flux. But newspeople know we want to be assured of progress, so they puff each discovery as a step toward human omniscience. As a result we are getting dizzy as we stumble down the twisting paths of our media nutritionists and child psychologists. In fact there is only one science really suited to daily editions—it's in the papers every day. Astrology.

EVIDENCE THAT IT TAKES SOME SOPHISTICATION TO READ AND REPORT ON SCIENCE

- *Chicago Tribune,* September 15, 1989: "Study: Lefties May Live Longer"
- *Chicago Sun-Times,* same day: "Southpaws Left to Ponder Earlier Death"

- *Detroit Free Press,* November 17, 1988: "Pill Doubles Heart Disease Risk, Study Finds"
- *Detroit News,* same day: "Encouraging News for Users of Pill"

Clearly, you've got to be careful which paper you subscribe to. It must have been treatment like this that confused the judge in New York:

- *New York Times,* August 15, 1989: "Judge Rejects DNA Tests"
- *New York Daily News,* same day: "Judge OKs DNA Tests for Court"

8

Polls,
Statistics
& Fantasy

- - - - - - - - - - - -

God cannot deal in statistics. This may surprise those of us who think of statistics as giving us something like omniscience, allowing us a global view of things. Statistics have become our ordinary mental fare. We see them in every newspaper. So why does God have trouble with them?

When you know everything, statistics become a restriction on your thought. To use them you have to ignore the details and reduce reality to just one aspect of the situation. That's why statistics work well with daily publication schedules. With so little space for the day's news, reporters use statistics to single out one part of reality for those of us who are impatient. We may feel enlightened to read that there are so-many-million registered Democrats, but if the truth were known, those people are not all that similar. It doesn't tax God to keep each one in mind; lumping cases together would mean forgetting the differences between them.

The other thing we need to relate to our reliance on statistics is that we newsreaders are woefully ignorant about the world. One would have thought that statistics would have helped educate us.

But journalists themselves have been commenting on this ignorance recently without taking responsibility for it. *Time* complained on March 28, 1994, that 72 percent of us didn't know the name of the ethnic group conquering Bosnia, 60 percent didn't know the group with which Israel had just signed a peace accord, 50 percent couldn't name the president of Russia, and 87 percent didn't know who Boutros Boutros-Ghali was. And those were precisely the stories *Time* had been covering! Of course we are totally ignorant of the tens of thousands of other stories that they don't cover. As are they.

So it is possible that the news's reliance on statistics actually makes us dumber than we would be if they didn't use them. Take an example from my local paper on August 16, 1989: "Parents, Teachers Split on Spanking." Seeing the headline, you might assume that the split mentioned was a split *between* the groups rather than *within* each group. Actually a Harris poll was reporting that 56 percent of teachers supported at least the possibility of physical punishment in schools whereas 53 percent of parents were against the practice. With a reported sampling error of 3 percent, the split might really have been exactly half and half. If that were the case, then the poll essentially indicated that there was no difference between the groups. But that would not be news. Conflict is news, so—you guessed it—the story put the issue in terms of conflict between teachers and parents. Conflict gets our attention.

Even if the media had not chosen to misrepresent the poll results, the poll was a falsification in itself. It suggested that there are two views of this subject. Anyone with any brain finds it very hard to answer pollsters' questions. Wouldn't you guess that there is a whole spectrum of thought on "physical punishment"? The question might have meant something different to everyone who responded. Most of the respondents probably tried to qualify their answers. None of those qualifications are part of the poll results, even though they may have been more important than the binary responses. Thus the polling company created a falsehood by forcing opinion into two categories. We now know *less* than we did before if we imagine the American public is divided into two camps on this subject. The irony is that we think statistics are showing an underlying reality when they actually are creating fables.

Statistics weren't invented for use in the news, of course. But the news is where they are most misleading. Social scientists recognize statistics as abstractions from reality. So they love to *debate* the figures. For lack of space and lack of sophistication, newspeople leave out the qualifications that scholars make. And unfortunately, when social scientists are put in the spotlight as experts, they begin to forget those qualifications themselves. Thus experts become the source for headlines such as "Liquor Is Quicker—on Women" (from my local paper). A headline like that will be remembered and repeated in family arguments without qualification, as if it were true of every woman and every man. Since the experts are not present at the dinner table, they cannot intervene and clarify.

Nothing is harder to read than a social science book filled with statistics, but nothing is easier to read than a news article that uses statistics. That is because social scientists know statistics need to be explained. Newsreaders may imagine that statistics "speak for themselves."

Sometimes the news misreads statistics so badly that it creates hoaxes. In the spring of 1992 the news reported an AIDS epidemic among American teenagers. CNN, PBS, the *New York Times,* the *Los Angeles Times, Newsweek* and *U.S. News & World Report* all headlined the problem, and the secretary of Health and Human Services rushed to announce a new ad campaign to warn teenagers. In fact, the number of teens diagnosed with AIDS had fallen from 170 in 1990 to 160 in 1991, according to the Center for Disease Control. The numbers for those aged twenty to twenty-four fell from 1,626 to 1,485. How did the news get it wrong? They believed a flawed report produced by the House Select Committee on Children, Youth and Families. Politicians love headlines and guaranteed themselves one by reporting a "62 percent rise" in two years. The figure was arrived at by combining 1990 and 1991 and comparing that with earlier years, masking the actual decline. The committee went on to cite two studies in the *Journal of the American Medical Association* that it had misread and that in fact contradicted the committee's alarmist conclusions.[1] It was an example of how a sensationalist press and eager politicians feed each other.

News Encourages Social Division

Statistics in the news often serve to divide us, which is worrisome, given the degree to which *USA Today* has popularized them. The newest division is between generations. News reports assign each of us to a generation (which it nicknames) and pits the generations against each other. We once thought of ourselves as divided by class, race and religion, but we decided it was not good to dwell on these differences. Yet news makes a big issue of very slight differences in the norms for the different age groups. (Remember, the statistics don't compare the whole groups' full ranges but only their means or averages.) It is part of the news's obsession with conflict.

Beyond that, statistics desensitize us in our relationships with each other. They screen out the puzzling and disordered details of human lives. Statistics treat people according to a binary arithmetic: the individual either is or is not whatever it is we're counting. So thinking in a statistical mode is not good for anyone who has to live in the real world and meet whole people.

The division between generations is a part of the news's obsession with the future. Dividing people according to age helps direct our attention toward the future, when they will have more news product to sell. But news also promotes division in general. For example, in my town there is a block-long concrete retaining wall that has become a community billboard especially favored by local college students. I have always loved that wall. It is remarkable how sweet-spirited the graffiti are—wishing a friend happy birthday or congratulations on graduation, pledging eternal love, memorializing someone who has died. Even as art some of it is striking. Our newspaper never took any notice of that wall until one day someone painted some rude remarks about gays and lesbians. Then the wall made the front page, with a picture. It was finally ugly enough to be news.

But I'm wandering. My point is that reaching for a global reality through statistics may teach us less than our neighborhood experience does. You may already have concluded this from failed political predictions that were based on statistics. We have all seen many editorial prophecies based on polling data that were later contradicted by events. During Margaret Thatcher's interminable government, every Labour party by-election victory was headlined as the first breath of spring. Each one was generalized into a general defeat for Thatcher's Toryism by confident—and mistaken—commentators. Of course one day they were bound to be right. And they would then want credit for being right, like astrologers who predicted something that finally came to pass.

The record of the Index of Leading Economic Indicators has also made us suspicious, because its prophecies are not always accurate. Economic figures, like the weather forecast, are one of the news elements people actually use in planning their lives. But we are beginning to realize how faulty they are. Take the figure for gross national product. We have all watched respectfully when that figure has flashed up on our TV screens. It seems like a very basic statement about our world. On April 26, 1988, the news reported that the U.S. GNP had grown 2.3 percent in the first quarter. A month later it had to report a slight correction in that figure: it was actually 3.9 percent. That is not a slight correction; it is a 70 percent change. Big investors would make very different plans depending on which of these figures was more accurate.

And what makes us confident that even the latter figure was accurate? Actual economists have serious doubts about much more specific indicators. Choose your favorite economist: Paul Samuelson, Nobel Prize winner, thinks that the Index of Leading Economic Indicators can give the *opposite* impression of economic trends. Allen Sinai doesn't trust the "trade-deficit figures." David Hall doubts the "retail sales report." Norman Robertson thinks the "capacity utilization figure" is misleading.[2] Apparently the closer you get to the ground, the less things resemble the figures that look so crisp in the news graphics.

Why does the news still use these statistical figures? Isn't it embarrassed to have to revise them so soon and so drastically? I suppose the answer is that news literally cannot get along without them. It must present everything briefly. It trades in prophecy—presenting everything as a trend—to remind us to buy tomorrow's issue. And it must flatter us with the illusion that we comprehend things almost as God does, circling the globe like a spy satellite, seeing whether anything has moved since yesterday. Newspeople can count on our forgetting the failed predictions.

Polls Replace Thinking
The point about flattering readers brings up another aspect of the use of statistics. You must have noticed how prevalent poll reports have become in our papers. We are getting to the point that every story in newsmagazines will include the results of a public opinion survey of what you, the customer, think of all this. And have you noticed that the spin of the story rarely goes against the results of the poll? That must make readers feel good. Opinion polls are the public talking back to the media. The industry sponsors them to assure itself that someone out there is listening and to judge what

kind of stories we want in tomorrow's edition. We can become *part* of the news by responding to the polls.

To that end, the polls make it easy for us. They never ask what we actually *know* about the issues, which would expose our lamentable ignorance. They ask only easy questions like, How do you feel about corruption in government, or the depletion of the ozone layer, or whether more should be done about crime? If they asked hard questions, they would run the risk of demonstrating how dumb we have become. What if they asked, "How much more would you guess it would cost you, per year, if manufacturers couldn't use pollutant X in your detergents and had to find another ingredient to do the same thing?" Or "Which rights would you be willing to give up to have crime stopped dead in its tracks here in Springfield?" Or "In four sentences or more, what is your definition of 'justice' (before I ask you about Senator X's proposal)?"

If news polls posed open-ended questions to get us to reveal our actual knowledge of any subject, responding to a poll would be a humbling experience. On January 26, 1998, *Time* reported that 64 percent of Americans (that is, of those who had time for this pollster) "acknowledge that Clinton has accomplished at least as much for the country as Reagan did, or more." That is a big thought. Did the pollster ask respondents to list thirteen accomplishments of each, and twelve failures, and assign each instance a weight for purposes of the final assessment? No historian would be ready to wade into those waters yet.

Incidentally, that was the week before the news began polling people about their feelings about Clinton's presidency in the light of new allegations about his sexual activities. You may remember that the polls on his "job performance" went up at that point. The journalists were surprised, to say the least, and a trifle annoyed. They had expected a lot of trouble for the president, which would sell a lot of news. So for once they were inclined to speculate about what that huge "approval rating" *meant* rather than to assume it meant he was suddenly discovered to be doing a better job.

Of course the responses could have meant something different for each person polled. I don't know how the question was worded, but some may have thought it was a joke or that their answer was a joke. Some, not being big fans of government, may have liked the idea that we would have an even weaker president. Others may have tried to specify that they thought Clinton was doing all right in foreign policy but not in fiscal policy. Some may prefer a president who is such an ordinary guy, whom they can feel sorry for.

But isn't it more likely that those poll responses had nothing to do with the president and everything to do with the press? Maybe most of those polled were saying, "We'd rather not hear about this. It's embarrassing. We don't need another of your everlasting investigations. Of course we'll have to read about it if you print it, but we're not gonna be happy about it." In other words, these are people who don't know they have a choice. They're trying to use their poll response to influence the news, when they could just stop the press—by canceling their subscription or changing channels. The lesson is that polls are no substitute for actual conversation with real people if our goal is understanding the world. Aggregating the figures from poll responses does not get you closer to understanding actual people.

News Disappears into Headlines

The big question is whether a *lack* of news has led to this decline in knowledge and interest or whether a *glut* of news is actually responsible. Certainly news headlines are more pervasive now than ever before. One doesn't need to go find them now; they confront us whether or not we ever buy a paper or make a ritual of watching CNN. We have more news product than ever, and it doesn't really register.

Our dumbness shows. A 1996 study of voter awareness would make you think that maybe many of those who *did* vote shouldn't have. Of a sample of people who voted in the 1996 election, only half knew that Newt Gingrich was Speaker of the House, and a quarter couldn't name the incumbent vice president. A third thought that President Clinton wanted bigger defense budgets than candidate Robert Dole did. A third were wrong about the direction of unemployment rates, half were wrong about the direction of the rate of inflation, and 70 percent were wrong about the direction of federal deficits. The respondents generally did have a couple of things right—perhaps by guessing.[3] But one has to wonder whether anything would be lost if the news corporations went out of business and we got our political information directly from competing local party offices.

Even if we don't vote, we seem happier than ever to share our opinions. One poll (*Time,* January 20, 1992) included a fictitious choice to see whether we know what we are talking about: 39 percent of those polled said they would not want any ethnic Wisians moving into their neighborhood. In fact, this fictional group proved to be one of the most unpopular of our ethnic groups.

Not only do we statistical-opinion-units give puzzling responses to silly questions, but we don't tell the truth about things we know for sure. Like whether we voted. After the 1994 congressional elections (*Time,* November 18, 1994), 56 percent of those polled said they had voted, when only 39 percent actually had. (Perhaps these steadily declining voter turnouts suggest that the news industry is making public affairs and politics a spectator sport.)

Polls are not designed to reveal our ignorance. But they regularly reflect badly on our judgment when reviewed at a later point. For example, in the presidential campaign of 1988 *Time* reported (September 14, 1987) that Senator Joseph Biden was particularly esteemed as "someone you can trust." He stood out among his fellow candidates in this regard, with 60 percent of respondents singling out this characteristic. A week later, revelations of plagiarism ended his candidacy.

The real "margin of error" in most polls is about 100 percent. The error is to think that we have any *thoughts* on most subjects. Of course we will have a *response*. For we just know that this kind pollster, looking modestly down at her clipboard, is really testing us. She secretly knows the right answer to the question and is only pretending to be indifferent to our answer. Naturally those who read the most news are those who will be the least likely to have views of their own. They will try the hardest to recall the attitudes they think informed people will have.

The media sponsor polls so that they will feel good and we will feel good. They let us know that our opinion is as important as any other part of the news (if we're in the majority). We let them know that we think they have chosen the right stories to get excited about. Unfortunately, their poll questions don't reveal our abysmal ignorance. And our poll responses are too much a matter of conditioning to have much to do with any real thinking we may be doing.

So we are increasingly confused about ourselves and our world. In a poll reported during the 1992 presidential campaign (*Time*, July 27, 1992) 66 percent of the sample responded that they were doing as well as or better than they were four years before. But 72 percent said that "the country" was definitely worse off. They had been following exasperated coverage of the Bush administration, no doubt, and couldn't connect the world of news with the world of real life. The former number represented the reality they knew, the latter the virtual reality of their news source.

CHAPTERS YOU HAVE BEEN EXPECTING BUT THAT ARE BEYOND OUR THEME

Spending time on all these themes would indeed increase the reasons for giving up on the news. But it would also suggest that the "problems" could be corrected, whereas I maintain that our knowledge and sanity depend on giving up news product.

- **"Ideological Bias Among Newspeople"**
  There are plenty of biased newspeople, but we are only dealing with the fundamental biases involved in marketing news product every day.
- **"Irresponsibility of Journalists"**
  Clearly becoming more common in response to the celebrification of TV newsreaders.
- **"Censorship"**
  A discussion of how prissy editors kill stories they would rather we didn't read.
- **"Incompetence of Reporters"**
  An increasing problem as their coverage becomes more ambitious.
- **"How TV Debases the Real News"**
  Only a matter of degree, since TV simply exaggerates the tendencies of all forms of periodical publication.
- **"How a Few Corporations Monopolize News"**
  Which does speed up the development of the news marketing that we have been discussing.
- **"How Much Worse Journalism Is in America Than in Other Countries"**
  Maybe, but only a matter of degree. Other countries follow us in spite of our sorry example. They have lagged because they

had a more elitist past, but as they accept the imperatives of
the bottom line we can expect them to adopt the methods that
have debased the product here.

9

Values,
Blame &
Nagging

We must be a strange lot. We seem to like being nagged about as much as we like being flattered. The news has found that worrying and blaming us works as well as deferring to us when it comes to getting us to buy their product. In the past people went to church to hear about their faults, and many decided they didn't like it. They started staying home on Sunday morning and reading the Sunday paper instead. Then the news started criticizing us. Of course news is not authorized to offer forgiveness, but it compensates by inviting us to join in blaming others.

I suppose that many of those who have kicked the news habit have done so because they are offended ("sick and tired," they would say) at being blamed for "everything." Real news junkies must not mind this play of guilt and self-righteousness, because it is a constant feature of the news as we know it. And yes, it has to do with the structural elements of daily publication.

The basis of morality is in taking sides or, more accurately, seeing all sides. Moral judgment begins with seeing things from another's point of view. (Remember the Golden Rule.) Newspapers could be very educational in this respect, yet they find it easier to identify some underdog groups and follow their fortunes. It takes less space in a newspaper, less time on the screen.

I have already noted that news cannot express respect. That is why it lacks any sympathy with religion, which is all about respect. (News only notices when religion does not show respect.) But news can express pity by making its readers feel guilty. If we are among the majority, after all, we are probably helping make things tough for the little guy. Identifying disadvantaged groups simplifies the task of news, making reports shorter and more straightforward. Discussing moral dilemmas would be complicated and often discouraging. It's easier for news to just keep score on who has slighted or supported one of the groups in its morality play.

Usually we are happy to side with underdogs, for at one time or another we have all felt that we were part of a minority. Now and then we realize that in certain respects we are part of an overbearing majority, and we are prepared to accept some scolding. The news takes advantage of this by encouraging the habit of siding against ourselves. But these scoldings may become too automatic, and it may dawn on readers that things are becoming one-sided.

For example, on May 7, 1990, *Time* had a cover story on how foul-mouthed and abusive our new crop of entertainers are. The article was typically ambivalent, not wanting to offend readers who might like this kind of entertainment but not wanting to alienate those who find it offensive either. In the final summary, however, the writer decided that there wasn't anything really wrong with this stuff: "It has always been the role of art to shock." (Art?) So the public should just get used to it. In case we hadn't gotten the point, on June 25 the magazine headlined a follow-up article about the *critics* of this art— "Anti-obscenity Campaigners Are Getting As Nasty As They Wanna Be"—so we would know who the bad guys are.

The odd thing about the original article was that it was *immediately* followed by a big article on "Bigots in the Ivory Tower." In this article we learned that some college students were insulting others or doing things that were considered disparaging to certain groups. The report was full of outrage. I was puzzled; what was the difference between these insults and the insults hurled by the entertainers? News justifies an entertainment culture that is filled with offensive gestures and cultural insults and then is surprised when people become offensive and abusive. Why didn't the editors see the connection? And why should they have had such opposite reactions?

Actually they were being perfectly consistent. In both cases the news put the majority in the wrong. The comedians were encouraged because they were reviling a majority group—white middle-class middle-Americans. And the students were scolded because they were part of the same majority. This goofy morality is what one has come to expect from the news. To grab the reader, news reports take sides. The easiest thing, apparently, is to side against ourselves. In many cases that may be the moral way. But if it becomes the invariable rule, readers will rarely notice.

Time did it again in its July 20, 1992, issue. On page 30 the magazine ran a story on Tipper Gore, wife of the vice president, belaboring her for her crusade against trash in rock lyrics. On the facing page they berated the Republican party for the trash in its political ads. Think about it: the trash they were attacking in the ads (references to sex and marijuana in anti-Clinton ads and to violence in ads using the Willie Horton case) is the same trash found in rock lyrics. Why are these things OK when produced for young people but evil when produced for grownups?

Why the News Takes Sides

Every now and then readers get tired of siding against themselves and talk about "bias in the news." But the problem goes deeper than the bias of writers; it may come from the short-circuited thinking I have just described. We expect to be criticized. We are honest enough to know we often deserve it. But majority groups get irritated when they realize that *only* they are being criticized and notice how careful the news is to not report anything negative about other groups.

Some groups are seldom praised, even when doing something right; other groups have a hard time catching any kind of criticism. When did you last see a story linking the handicapped, single mothers, homosexuals or journalists with such topics as child molestation, child abandonment, shoplifting or delinquent bill-payment? But it wouldn't surprise us to see such stories about scout-masters, priests or police officers. As the joke goes, the *Washington Post*'s last headline will read "World Ends; Women and Minorities Hurt Worst."

Our earlier discussion of how news drives science suggested the reason the news never reports studies of the social pathologies (moral failings) of its favored groups. No such studies are done. Social scientists want to be famous. You wouldn't get famous by showing that Native Americans are twice as likely as other groups to abuse animals (a purely made-up statistic). But if you were the one who discovered that antiabortion activists abused their pets, that might earn you fifteen minutes of fame. The National Science Foundation doesn't want headlines screaming that it funded research into the failings of social underdogs. It might be enlightening. It might even be useful knowledge. But it wouldn't encourage Correct Thinking.

Once in a while the news obviously goes over the top. In early 1993 the *Washington Post* ran a story in which evangelist Pat Robertson's followers were called "poor, uneducated, and easy to command." There was some complaint. Would the *Post* ever even *think* of using similar words to describe some sect of African Americans? If Robertson himself had used those terms about anyone, newspeople would have treated it as an example of his notorious insensitivity.

The Power of the Press

In short, we've all become part of a conspiracy. Newspeople know that to pass criticism around evenly might ease the guilt of the sucker majority who are their customers. Conscience is the only lever that the news has to get public support for Correct Thinking. Doubtless you have heard the phrase *the power of the press.* The media's power over us is the guilt I have been describing. For the last several generations it has been the news and not the churches that has cultivated this guilt.

It would be a rare newspaper that didn't have stories or at least editorials that implied that we American taxpayers aren't doing enough for somebody. Such pieces function like a passing of the collection plate. How about the recent hurricane victims in Honduras, or the Moldavians who want to emigrate to Romania, or the drought victims in Mali, or parents who want reliable, stimulating, loving, public-funded daycare for their children? It is important for the news to keep worrying us about something, working on our guilt a little every day, rubbing us sore. That is how one becomes sensitive. And it's got to be repeated daily.

How many stories have you seen that begin "Pressure is building on A to do B," meaning that "we intend to keep running stories on this until we hound A into doing B." It's like saying, "Either you do what we want (about gun control, college football playoffs, higher gasoline taxes) or we will drive everyone crazy with this." Another favorite is "This story will just not go away," as in "Accusations of A against Senator B, though regularly denied, will just not go away." Which translates as "We hope that you share our

obsession with this and will want more editions on the subject."
(Of course you *can* make the story go away by turning off the tube;
I'll offer instructions on that later.)

The idea that the news keeps nagging us seems to contradict what
I have said earlier about its jumpy attention span. But the subject,
the focus, can change every week. It's the tone that prods us along
and proves the power of the press. Nagging serves to help create
change, so that the news will have more to report. If newspeople
want a change of government, they will keep calling the current
government a "regime." If they object to a particular official, they
will not call him by his title, which would suggest legitimacy, but
may call him a "strongman." They may be a little arbitrary here;
arrangements they approve of are referred to as "the law of the
land," but those they want changed are "present regulations." They
may point out that the Supreme Court has frequently reversed
itself—when reporting a ruling that they disapprove—but express
satisfaction at other decisions, which they call "definitive." Attitudes the press hopes to change are said to "persist," meaning that
they are taxing some editor's patience.

News as Caricature

All of this—the simplistic moralizing and the nagging tone—
comes to a focus in the political cartoon. You may know that the
New York Times doesn't usually print political cartoons. Its editors
have some sense that caricature reduces the dignity and even the
truthfulness of the news. But when you think about it, the news is
caricature by its very nature. Certainly there are degrees in these
matters—there is more responsible and less responsible journalism.
But at best the news simplifies our view of every kind of reality to
the point of distortion, and cartoons only show this at its most
squalid.

The cartoon completes the news. Its purpose is not to inform but to emotionalize the issues by making them grotesque. Those who don't know how they feel about recent events can find out by looking at the political cartoon. Its effect is to boost us above our leaders by reducing their scale, lest we become too respectful of authority. The tragedy is that we triumph too effortlessly. Once we've checked out the political cartoon each day, we see no need for further action. Those leaders have already been put down by that outrageously funny drawing. After all, it was in the place of honor in the newspaper, the most prominent thing on the editorial page.

So cartoons take the place of political action in the same way that the old holidays of "inversion" did for medieval peasants. A couple of times a year the lower orders were allowed to pretend that they were kings or bishops or great ladies and might actually be allowed to lord it over their masters or ridicule them. This let the steam out of social protest. Similarly, no sooner have we elected our new leaders than we have caricatures that put them in their place. Every day we are treated to this inversion, watching our masters stand in the pillory among the editorials. Obviously this hasn't prevented the growth of a big, unresponsive government. The real government—the permanent bureaucracy—doesn't make very funny cartoons. Its powers grow to suit itself, while we are amusing ourselves elsewhere.

Groups as well as individuals can be ridiculed in political cartoons if they are not an important share of the market. Over the years caricature has done much to energize conservative voters and justify the outlook of religious groups that have felt unfairly treated. When right-wing talk radio began, the guardians of Correct Thinking were aghast to hear another side and redoubled their efforts to censor it. The frustration of a Right that had long had no voice led it to caricature its opponents in kind. So we don't have a lot of civil discourse in this country. Maybe there is some at the local level, but news discourse makes it difficult.

The news's simplification of complex issues is a form of caricature not of people but of positions. We see this, for example, when the news treats an ethical debate as a political issue. Take the abortion "debate," the one we are all most familiar with. News treatment tends to reduce this ethical-legal debate to just two sides not only to save space but also to sharpen the sense of conflict that energizes readers. Journalists may allude to the fact that there is a moral dimension to the issue, but there is no space for arguments for the various positions. So the news shifts to the politics of the issue, asking not what these people think but what is their voting strength, and what are their tactics.

News wants the story to continue. So the larger issue is lost in an endless series of lesser demands—whether abortion must be done with the spouse's consent, or at the taxpayers expense, or with parental consent, or with parental notification, or with counseling and so on. At each of these escalating steps, again only two sides are presented. True moral dilemmas are uncomfortable, often involving conflicting rights and no-win situations. So we prefer being invited to side wholeheartedly with one party in these skirmishes. And the cartoonists will help by drawing pictures that "dittoheads" will think are funny.

You watch. All our debates over constitutional amendments will sink in this way. These debates cannot be decided on the basis of present law because they deal with what the law should be. They ought to be argued out in the higher reaches of justice and morality. In chapter three we discussed how a secular culture is reduced to counting heads in lieu of debating. So the news rushes on to the political level to see which side can force the issue by superior numbers.

The only thing worse than watching the news caricature moral issues is watching it parade its concern for the ethical-issue-of-the-season. News will follow the politicians who have recently seized the high ground on some previously ignored outrage. Or it will report the moral views of our celebrities so that we will know what some soap-opera star thinks of the future of marriage, for example. But the industry gives the game away every New Year when *Time* magazine names its Person of the Year. For the next month *Time* keeps busy trying to justify its choice, especially when it had to name some world-troubler. Actually newspeople are perfectly right to pick these obnoxious and immoral tyrants. Such figures are creating the change that equals news.

The general public cannot seem to remember that that is what news is. Readers will complain that surely a Person of the Year should be an admirable character, a positive force. They don't accept the magazine's protest that it never said that this was their favorite person but only the most newsworthy. At that point some exasperated reader can be counted on to write in, "Well what can we expect from a magazine that named Hitler its Man of the Year in 1938?"

We cannot quite absorb the idea that news is what upsets us or upsets the world. If we wanted to read about acts of moral decency, we have come to the wrong place. Moral decency is very rarely news. That is because it is expected and common—in real life. It will become less common as life comes to imitate news.

FOR THE PUZZLE PAGE

• *Cincinnati Post,* August 5, 1989: "Drug Gangs Invading Ohio"

• *Cincinnati Enquirer,* same day: "Few Outsiders in Local Drug Trade"

• *Hollywood Reporter,* March 15, 1989: "CBS Records Drops Most Vinyl"

• *Variety,* same day: "CBS Disks Reaffirms That It's Still in the Vinyl Biz" (reporting on a press conference that CBS called to clarify its position)

FOR THOSE WHO HAVE BEEN MISSING THE *NEW YORK TIMES* AND *WASHINGTON POST*

• *New York Times,* August 23, 1993: "In a Shift, U.S. Sees Wider Somalia Role to Stop Clan Leader"

• *Washington Post,* same day: "Exit Plans For Somalia Stepped Up"

• *New York Times,* June 8, 1995: "Greenspan Sees Chance of Recession"

• *Washington Post,* same day: "Recession Is Unlikely, Greenspan Concludes"

10
Deep Theory
News as Culture Substitute

Something peculiar is happening to us, and journalists themselves have some inkling of it. I've quoted a number of reports that point out how ill-informed we are, how seldom we vote and how our interest and trust in the news is declining. Newspeople seem to think that the cure for all this is more news consumption; I think the cure will start with less. Ignoring the news won't cure us if we don't make some better use of our minds, but it is a necessary first step. News is addictive, and if we want to regain an active intelligence, it will mean getting over the idea that news keeps us informed in any grown-up sense of that term.

There are many things these days that interfere with the higher mental functions—with concentration, analysis, wonder. But the greatest irony in our situation is that even our primary information supply—our periodical news—contributes to the decline of our intellectual culture. In his searching critique of the news industry's irresponsibility, James Fallows lamented that it no longer helped us "to see life steady and see it whole."[1] It never did. It can't. The very survival of the news business depends on our seeing life as jumpy and scattered.

Social scientists sometimes emphasize how societies are held together by our communications media—more than by economic institutions or political institutions or police. So naturally social theorists like Jürgen Habermas worry about whether the media are falling into the wrong hands—whether they are biased or irresponsible or incompetent or whether they are serving somebody's hegemonic agenda. These theorists are missing the point. We should be worrying about the very *structure* of our communications, specifically their periodical scheduling.

Those same social philosophers point out that "primitive" societies are held together by their cultures. They mean *culture* in the sense of all the ways of thinking and living that people teach their children. This difference between culture and news is fundamental. Cultures are relatively settled. The word *culture* originally described agriculture, the cultivation of something that grew, slowly. But news is relatively unsettled in all the ways we've discussed. News doesn't want things to seem settled if it means we would lose our appetite—our addiction—to news product.

A news industry is not a necessity of life. A lot of people in our "advanced" societies do without it, hearing only snatches of the media's haphazard selection of subjects. I run into such people all the time, even around universities, when they realize that it is safe to admit this to me. But culture is a necessity of life or at least of society. Yet most of those who are in charge of our society's affairs think that news is the *most* important thing to know, if one can judge by their reading habits. They seem to think of it as a substitute for culture. They imagine that it is a sort of substitute for books, a shortcut to wisdom. It is not. News is the opposite of books; it is an inoculation against culture and reflection.

Before there was a news industry—when news came along irregularly and informally—societies were held together by their cultures. People shared fairly settled assumptions about what was reasonable, natural, expected or good. Scholars use various terms to describe this situation, speaking of *master texts, metanarratives, myths* (without the pejorative connotation of untruth) or *ideologies.* Usually these terms betray a distrust of culture, as scholars point out how they bind our thought. Culture is a prison in their view. We aren't absolutely free as long as we are unconscious of the cultural constraints on our thinking.

No doubt that is true. But what *absolute* freedom would mean is something of a puzzle. Do we constantly have to think of more and more outrageous things to do to prove we are free of all constraints? Feodor Dostoyevsky's *Crime and Punishment* is the most famous portrayal of the nihilistic absurdity, if not insanity, of the notion of absolute freedom. Do we need to search out all our customs and traditions and root them out just because they are customary and traditional? Must they be destroyed so that each of us may recreate things as we feel the need?

All this probes the deeper question of whether we are primarily individuals or primarily members of societies. Does the question surprise you? If you have trouble thinking of yourself as primarily an element within a society, try thinking how many hours you would last on your own in a jungle. And yet the media and our media-driven institutions have tricked us into assuming that society is only a convenience. This is shortsighted; we can't enjoy the benefits of society without generally submitting to its forms. But the news is so corrosive to social and cultural standards that it has begun to create a dysfunctional situation in which people don't want to vote, like to "trash" their culture, and are contemptuous of civility. The industry is caught in the position of sponsoring a continuous referendum on our cultural inheritance.

If a society is to function in meeting our individual needs, there must be a considerable measure of agreement. It won't be perfect agreement, but there will at least be a language in which the disagreement can be carried on and perhaps resolved. This "language" includes more than words and grammatical rules. It includes shared assumptions, common metaphors, "legendary" models and a scaling of values. In short, we speak to each other through a shared culture. The scholars who want to look at these cultures through a telescope cannot be our guides to living. They are right to point out the dangers of culture, but these are the dangers of being social.

Before the news industry came into being, the Bible served as the master text in English and American culture. This did not imply that everyone had a devout *belief* in the Bible, but it did mean that people were familiar with its stories and metaphors and its ways of structuring moral and social reality. It served this purpose for illiterates and philosophers alike. This culture could produce an Abraham Lincoln without the benefit of formal schooling, but only with a familiarity with Scripture. Though Lincoln never formally joined a church, his mind had been shaped by the one book available to him as he read it and heard it quoted. As president he didn't need a speechwriter when it came time for him to speak for the country. And yet out of the rhetoric of that culture he wrote some of the classic compositions in the English language.

This skill is not taught in college these days, and certainly not in journalism departments. Classic lines would be slashed through with blue pencil, because news discourse calls for something else—something instantly disposable. A newspaper that you wanted to save would have failed in its objective, which is to lead to the next newspaper.

The news has been trashing Lincoln's cultural heritage for three centuries now by trying to keep it always in question. News plows up the ground under our feet. When editors discover that we are taking something for granted, it becomes another item to put in play. And we have foolishly accepted the idea that we should take nothing for granted but should become relentlessly and entirely self-conscious. This would mean continually reinventing our consciousness, and we could not survive the effort.

Religion and the news find themselves in fundamental conflict because they represent opposite poles in their attitudes toward human life. So this conflict is not because journalists are irreligious, although if one believes the studies on this topic, journalists are on average noticeably less religious than their readers. The basic incompatibility is that religion celebrates what we believe to be settled and even eternal, while the news has a problem with that. Spirituality is the opposite of news consciousness.

Trashing religion is such a pervasive part of our media that it goes unnoticed in some circles. In my doctor's office I picked up *Newsweek* for March 27, 1995, and found religion treated at five points. There was an admiring review of an anti-Catholic movie, *Priest,* an admiring review of a book on snakehandlers in Alabama (alone among the hundred books that appeared that week) and the news that the Mormons had picked an "aged" man to be president (not surprising given their seniority rules). Then a columnist reported on a fifteenth-century book in which, she asserts, "the words 'witch' and 'woman' were used synonymously throughout." This inspired numerous reflections on churches in the twentieth century and was used to plug her own hard-hitting novel on the subject. And finally, there was a report on weeping religious statues in Italy.

This really is the news of religion—the weirdness. After all, it is not really news when religion heals hearts or homes or inspires soup kitchens, medical missions, rehabilitation programs or artistic and publishing projects. These things are expected. People may object to the way news treats religion because it is all they ever hear about religion, and they know it's unfair. But why is news all they read? They should know by now that news isn't a reflection of the world but only of what has gone wrong in the world.

And this inspires our culture wars—conflicts fought between

those who think cultural traditions tap into something transcendent and those who think such talk only justifies the status quo. Those on the Right, which the news correctly calls the Religious Right, don't like to see unrelenting challenges to everything they hold to be right or good or natural. But news can't help challenging the old in the interest of the new. Because the public takes in very little that is not news product, it finds the playing field tilted steeply toward change. Of course things don't develop very well when we keep pulling them up to check their roots. One has to wonder how much our social dysfunctions are the result of the hypertrophy of news when we do not balance it with more settled culture and commitments.

News never asked to replace culture. Its proper function is to raise questions about dominant ideas, not to become the dominant discourse, silencing or undermining all others. It is not natural for it to destroy those metanarratives, for it cannot replace them. Since periodical publication must always give priority to the new, it continuously deconstructs itself. Thus the news can never be a substitute for the traditional cultures about which it creates a generalized suspicion.

Any culture can become so heavy as to depress the spirit and block the spontaneity that keeps it alive. On the other hand, tradition is the wisdom of past generations, and the soil from which innovation grows. Tradition is a larger democracy, including generations that have gone before and assuming some responsibility for generations to come. It is one thing to build on traditional culture and reform or reshape it. It is quite another to hear only that which is new.

But one might see the present news industry as being in noticeable decay. The widely lamented deterioration of our news product may be because it is no longer part of a larger culture—of books, discussion (not watching discussion but engaging in it) and quiet reflection. In the high-stakes competition between news outlets, news's entertainment character has become egregious, disgusting, laughable. Our media cannot seem to ignore the freakish and the deviant, the obscene and outrageous. Tendencies that have always been in news discourse are becoming more obvious as industry accountants refine their calculations of the bottom line.

True conservatives and true radicals should both applaud the decline of the news industry as a (flawed) means of social bonding. Both would argue that the consciousness industry entrenches the hated bureaucratic and commercial establishment. And both would say that it erodes the social and cultural practices that could give meaning and beauty to life. In his book *The Cultural Contradictions of Capitalism,* Daniel Bell points out the lack of fit between the institutional and cultural sides of modern life. Although he ignored the media, he did describe the sorry plight of a society in which compulsive and unsatisfying work is only compensated by compulsive and unsatisfying indulgence. Yet it is precisely the media that divert attention from the weight of our institutions even while they churn our culture. The result is a restless politics, a trashy culture and irresponsible social relations.

One can see the damage in our educational institutions. They now take their cue from the media and suppose that they exist for the purpose of challenging received ideas. The study of literature, for example, is no longer to encourage appreciation or enthusiasm so much as analysis and suspicion. Schools were begun for the purpose of passing on what was valuable in the culture, but the list of those things is shrinking. Instead of emphasizing content and understanding they now focus on skills.

Don't get me wrong. I am not asking the media to become more respectful toward what I am calling "culture." Fostering respect is simply not the purpose of the news. The habits of news consciousness—criticism, suspicion, attention to the mundane and the pre-

sent—are vital. But they have become tyrannical in their domi-
nance, destroying creativity, appreciation, responsibility. We need
both these modes but are open only to one.

After many years of assuming that periodical media make modern societies possible, we need to consider whether news consciousness is making these societies impossible. Are our societies
becoming so "overdeveloped" that they can no longer do the things
that societies must do? For instance, can we successfully educate
our children when we cannot seem to agree on a curriculum that
could be stigmatized as traditional? What can schools do when all
that school-board members know is what they read in the papers?

Can we socialize children when family patterns are in constant,
even daily, dispute? Keep in mind that no such debate will ever be
concluded as long as the industry must market another issue tomorrow.

Can news addicts suspend political campaigning between elections long enough to cooperate with the people's choice? Or must
there be a daily referendum on what appears to be happening?

Can we manage social debates over the months or years that it
may take for our judgment to mature, or must the debates be settled
before news readers lose interest? And will we be able to involve a
real range of voices in these debates, or must we all be forced into
dubious dichotomies for the sake of journalistic drama?

One cannot prove historically how much the news industry has
contributed toward making the world a worse or a better place. If asked
whether the civil rights movement would have been possible without
media pressure, one could only reply that the media existed for several
centuries before that movement began, doing other things: starting the
Spanish-American War, encouraging the appeasement of Hitler.[2] If
one wanted to argue centuries, the news-driven twentieth century
would be the clear leader in sheer human bestiality. But there are many
causal factors to be considered, of course.

In the end the question we must ask ourselves is whether we could use news for the very limited purposes for which it is suited, without imagining that the real world fits into a half-hour frame. We cannot ask the media to reform; it is operating according to its nature. What we could ask is that consumers recognize the periodical press for what it is and realize our dependence on the more settled cultures the news constantly questions. At its inception no one dreamed that the news would ever be thought of as an adequate substitute for culture. But like a bad currency it has driven out things with a better claim to our attention.

QUOTES TO STITCH ON A SAMPLER

Nothing can now be believed which is seen in a newspaper. Truth itself becomes suspicious by being put into that polluted vehicle. ... I really look with commiseration over the great body of my fellow citizens, who, reading newspapers, live and die in the belief that they have known something of what has been passing the world of their time. ... The man who never looks into a newspaper is better informed than he who reads them; inasmuch as he who knows nothing is nearer to truth than he whose mind is filled with falsehoods and errors.
THOMAS JEFFERSON

If you watch TV news, you know less about the world than if you just drink gin out of a bottle.
GARRISON KEILLOR

11

Virtual
Society or
Real Community?

This is the point at which other media critics would make their recommendations on how the media should change its ways. But I have taken the view that the worst feature of the news is its essential feature—its timeliness. So really, it can't be fixed. Periodical publication has tendencies that defeat the best intentions of editors. What should we recommend, then? That we censor the press or close it down because it is a mental-health hazard? That we nationalize the networks or set term limits for editors?

The easy answer is that we don't need to do anything at all about the news. We can let the industry go about its business and just not buy its product. We will all want to read it occasionally, of course, when something interesting is going on. You might worry that an undercapitalized industry would not be able to do its job. But there will always be a few people who need to fill empty lives with news product. Even today, much of our news is written right off "press releases" and "briefings." The well-funded news industry's contribution sometimes seems to be little more than adding a tone of suspicion.

We certainly don't need to get into the issue of freedom of the press. It is worth pointing out, however, that this freedom originally referred only to books and pamphlets.[1] In the more intellectual milieu of the eighteenth century, people thought newspapers were too sketchy to convey ideas. So they let them say whatever they liked. Meanwhile they went to books and pamphlets (quarterlies, in today's terms) for the extended thinking that was so much more important.

I should also point out that I am not recommending that we give up news product as much as I am pointing out that this is already happening. I'm just trying to explain why it's happening and why we don't need to be apologetic about it. News served a useful purpose when culture and society were too monolithic and people needed to get their heads out of the clouds. In the last three hundred years the balance has shifted and the danger is on the other side. My recommendation is that news be put in its place, perhaps on a monthly schedule but in more substantial amounts, and that it be read *after* we've read more substantial fare, if there's time.

The other part of my recommendation is that we rebuild our communities to replace the virtual society that the news industry fabricates. If you still think of the news's world as real, try thinking whether you could produce a parody of its worldview. Parodying it would make you more aware of its conventions. Could you, in fact, parody the *New York Times*'s pinhole-world paradigm? Ask yourself which points of view would be shocking in their stories. Whom do they treat with respect, and whom do they dismiss or ridicule? Who are consulted as experts? Why do they identify some issues as moral and others as political? Above all, on which issues and events are they silent, indicating the boundaries of the news cosmos?

Politics Without News
Still, you may be thinking, what would become of our politics if

our media languished? Would we be able to mobilize public opinion when we need to throw the rascals out? Well why do we still have so many rascals after all these years of a news industry? The news does throw people out, it is true. But it throws out the good as often as the bad. (Think about the presidential primary system, for instance.) It is obvious that news has not necessarily energized us politically. The percentage of people who vote is in a long-term decline. Having to watch politicians posture and display themselves before the media may have given us the urge to switch them off.

The political change in Eastern Europe in the late 1980s did not come about with the assistance of a free press. They had rumors. We often make a distinction between rumor and real news, as if the latter were certified safe. But has that been your experience? In the cases where you have been personally involved with a news story, were you impressed by the accuracy of the report? Isn't it odd that we trust the news to cover a typhoon in Bangladesh when we know it can't get the local school-board issue straight?

Investigative reporting also may actually go better if informants think their information will become part of a comprehensive, extended treatment and not dribbled out in headline-grabbing bits. The calculated leaking of little, often misleading facts to the press might stop. If we were to buy quarterly journals or whole books on our society's functions or malfunctions, we would become more mature critics. In other words, dropping the commercial news may be necessary in order to *become* informed, in a more mature understanding of the term.

Maybe you still don't feel right about this. If we just ignore all those subjects that the news brings to our attention, how would we ever sustain the concern needed to deal with the issues of our time? Alas, that is just my point. The news doesn't keep anything before our attention. It jumps around to *follow* our attention. Editors try acid rain, to see whether that interests us, and then nuclear proliferation, date rape, airline safety, automobile recalls, genocide and cloning. With reports on four of these today, another four tomorrow, what is the chance that we will see progress on any of them? Wouldn't you expect the opposite? Perhaps the reason we don't see more progress is that the news reports create a feeling of concern that fully satisfies our public spirit. If we read about things in the kind of depth that the muckraking magazines offered, might we actually do something more intelligent about them?

Active citizenship should mean individuals concentrating on the affairs that involve them and that they can influence—that is, local issues. If more local issues were being addressed, there might not be as many national ones. Early sociologists like Robert Park who tried to make sense of institutionalized news concluded that it wasn't there to inform us, really, but to initiate face-to-face discussion. It was the discussion rather than the subject discussed or the conclusion reached that had a bonding effect.

We think of the news as primarily an information source. But at a deeper level the news is a form of society. For some of us the news is where we live: our identities are found in the periodicals we read and the programs we watch rather than in the places we live or the people we associate with. We may "know" the people in the news better than we know the people in our apartment building. We may even use the news as an escape from our neighbors and the drabness of our lives.

What if we plunged into our own lives instead? What if we neglected the celebrity gossip, political rehash, distant natural disasters and plane crashes and started cultivating our own neighborhoods? We would no longer have the feeling of omniscience that comes from surveying the whole world from a satellite transmission. We might lose the feeling of superiority we get from seeing caricatures of the unprogressive elements in our population. And we would miss vicariously rubbing shoulders with the beautiful people. But we could make our own neighborhoods more beautiful. We could become much better informed about the views of people around us who would never get to finish their sound bites in local news. And we might make common cause with people the media have made us suspicious of.

Hiding from the World?

Still, you wonder, how can we simply hide from the wider world and pretend it isn't there? Remember, we are already ignoring almost everything that goes on in the world. Look at today's front page, and then kick back and think of all the countries in the world, all the cities and all the towns in your state and all the industries, universities, churches, charities, movements, arts and laboratories where something interesting might be going on. Even the news industry is unaware of the stories available to them, because they only follow a dozen or so, which you've shown you will pay for.

So you might object that you don't want to know everything. I agree. The things we actually need to know are very few. And they don't fall into the category of news. If we have to ignore something, it ought to be the ephemeral. What we need to concentrate on are what we suspect are the great truths, the age-old topics. We don't seem worried about ignoring these. We have things exactly backward. We do need common topics to have something to talk to each other about, but those topics needn't be the current world outlaws, tycoons, actresses or athletes.

Think of the really solid communities that still exist. Are they the big media markets? Wouldn't you guess that it would be quite the reverse? The media only simulate society for people who don't have the real thing. And this pseudosociety doesn't work. There may be so little real community in the big media markets that people are afraid to venture outside, and so they watch the news from China instead. James Fallows offers a number of accounts of how newspapers have actually helped rebuild communities instead of simply spreading cynicism. But his examples are all about local situations and local news.[2] Fallows seems to assume that this could be translated to national affairs by a national media, but I doubt it. When societies reach a certain size they cease to be societies, whatever the communications technology available to news corporations.

In the 1880s Joseph Pulitzer, the famous publisher, figured out that his urban papers existed primarily to sell advertising space, not to spread the news. Newspapers could increase the rates for their advertising space by increasing their circulation, and they could increase circulation by sensationalizing their news. So the news became the advertising for his papers—actually the advertising for his advertisements![3] Pulitzer's papers bragged about having the news faster, fuller and more colorful than their rivals. Eye-grabbing layouts, pictures, headlines, cartoons and simple sentences all helped sales. These papers were the main reading of the immigrant population in American cities. They were a textbook in American life for those just off the boat. The news did not need to tell them about high politics or diplomacy, it just needed to show them how Americans talked and what Americans bought.

Nothing has changed in a century except that we have all become immigrants. We're not comfortable with our past and feel like travelers to the future. We are afraid that when we arrive, we won't know anyone. The news offers to fill us in. Like immigrants, we are ashamed of the traditions and dress that we have brought with us. We want to be told what's going on and what attitude to take toward it. That's why we'll need another paper tomorrow.

Beginning Your Education

So how can you, personally, learn to inhabit your world instead of just observing it? Let's not think about what we all must do. That is the way of the news—addressing us in the anonymous voice of an imagined public, confident that we will all want to get in step. Accept the fact that we are diverse and that you must find the community and culture in which you are most truly at home.

As surely as you need human contact, you need food for thought. News is not the answer, but if you give it up cold turkey, you will need something to fill the void. There will be withdrawal symptoms. You could try a news diet—a few nibbles of it between large helpings of something more substantial—until your color improves. Biographies would be a good place to begin. Get a taste for the whole story, not just a daily slice. Even the biography of a celebrity is instructive if taken whole, as opposed to the gossip that keeps celebrities afloat in the news. Go on to broader histories. Not political histories necessarily, but the history of whatever interests you.

Soon you will graduate to more searching discussions of issues that have only been touched on in the news. Somewhere between a weekly and a monthly schedule, one passes from excitement to reflection. You can follow the discussion of public-policy questions in quarterly publications. This is also periodical literature, of course, and is subject to a little of that faddishness, but it's much less toxic than dailies or weeklies. And quarterlies have the advantage that they come in all political flavors. Try a variety to find out who you are.

You won't have to give up reading about world problems. In fact, as you get into whole books, you'll be amazed at how little the news taught you about the world you live in. Nor will you have to give up a daily paper to begin your therapy, since there is so much other than news in them. There are the comics. And there is sports coverage, when it is actually about athletic contests and not just salary negotiations. Recipes, reviews, gardening tips—there's no reason to give all this up. Even the ads may be useful. This would be sufficient material for considerable discussion. Use the front page to line the birdcage, for fear that you'll imagine that it will make you informed. So what if you aren't up on things? At least you won't be caught repeating the news that toilet seats can't transmit genital warts when tomorrow's edition is about to inform us that they can after all.

Some of our holistic therapists have raised eyebrows by instructing patients to restrict their news intake. I suppose they are referring to the news industry's obsession with conflict. No doubt many of us have discovered this on our own. I have also suggested that it would be morally healthy to give up watching and reading news, given the damage that confrontational media do to civil discourse.

It may worry some of us that the community life I am promoting tends by its nature to be religious. As Jean-Jacques Rousseau recognized, all social contracts are religious at their base. By definition, real community or society is based on some sort of ultimate agreement. We must be able to appeal to transcendent standards of justice if our justice is to be more than the will of the stronger. Our communities must also be able to ask for a measure of individual sacrifice if they are to be held together by anything other than naked power.

Religion in this sense has been in an unequal struggle with a news discourse that corrodes any notion of the eternal or of human integrity. It is unequal because the news will lose. As we see it self-destructing, we may fear for any "societies" that are only held together by their news consciousness. But something more elemental will survive. It would not be a tragedy if these revitalized communities turned out to be recognizably Christian or Jewish or Buddhist or even more in the line of ethnic traditionalism or civil religion, for the more secularized among us. The important thing to remember is that all community is local. That is why all this is bad news to news corporations and their earnings reports.

In the meantime, religion should not try to get into the news or try to tame it. Instead it should offer another kind of discourse in the place of a flawed news discourse—one that does not shrink from discussion or responsibility. We all know the dangers that can accompany religious discourse. It is dinned into us daily. What we need to be reminded of are the dangers of its suppression.

What About the Younger Generation?

The generation growing up now is less likely to watch the news on television and much less likely to read newspapers than people did thirty years ago. Beyond that, the amount of news in the average paper or broadcast has declined very substantially, and our trust in this news is diminishing. I could quote statistics on these points if I hadn't disparaged them earlier. But you can't help having noticed that journalism is dwindling to the one big story of the day. Now the news industry and its intellectual proponents will naturally respond, "But look how ill-informed the younger generation is already. Are you seriously proposing that they need *less* news?" Yes.

I believe that our ignorance is generally the result of the news's crowding out other intellectual activities—on the part of not just the young but also those who should have been teaching the young. News is now broadcast twenty-four hours a day, and national newspapers are on sale all over the country. Test scores of all sorts go down. What the rising generation needs are books. Grown-up books. Parents and schools shy away from challenging children with anything they might grumble about and may think that news is the next best thing. But one does not graduate from news to books. News inoculates one against books by fostering the impression that with news you can know everything, or enough anyway.

The young will need to be weaned to something more solid. This will not be easy. A decline of news consumption will not necessarily mean a decline in news consciousness. You can be in the grip of the day's big story without having sat through a newscast and imagine that you are "informed." A generation raised on news will not automatically turn to something more substantial. For if there is one lesson they have absorbed, it is that becoming informed should not require an effort. But we can hope that their attention will become more local. We are social beings, and this may point toward some kind of cultural rebirth. It will be local and primitive at first, but it may foster a greater sense of cultural responsibility than can be conveyed by a news-and-entertainment business.

Politicians are worried about any decline of news consumption. If there were a general boycott of news, it seems likely that government would step in and try to save the news business. Congress has considered several measures that would make the coverage of political campaigns more complete. Bills have been introduced that would require bigger sound bites, a year of tax-payer-funded coverage of presidential candidates, and requirements for the networks to donate time to the parties.[4] The news industry is offering to help here too. Having created a politics of incessant opposition and confrontation—instead of discussion and deliberation—the news now talks of creating "watchdogs." They would monitor the unfair statements of their own ads, which in turn pay for their news.

Ben Bradlee of the *Washington Post* (of all people) once quoted Thomas Jefferson (of all people) as saying that the "man who never looks into a newspaper is better informed than he who reads them, inasmuch as he who knows nothing is nearer the truth than he whose mind is filled with falsehood and error."[5] Jefferson was president when he said this, and he was having a bad day. But if he had pursued that thought, he might have concluded that what the country needs is a free press that we don't necessarily feel we have to pay attention to.

I wish I could be more confident that disenchantment with the ephemeral world of news will be compensated by a growing taste for something more solid. One cannot be entirely hopeful on that score; the damage we have sustained through news addiction is great. But you could test yourself: pick up a book today and start some mind building. Read something you bought a while ago, or go back to the bookstore. Quit parroting the news, and your neighbors will notice your new, more solid self. Right now your brain is like a sieve with the news pouring through. Start reading something substantial, and you'll lose all interest in watching journalists write in the sand.

I remember arriving at work one day and finding a colleague standing in front of the *New York Times* vending machine, looking baffled. He had put in his money and pulled out . . . yesterday's edition! Today's hadn't yet arrived. He expected sympathy. But I wondered what the matter was. Yesterday that edition would have been just fine—probably a high point in his routine day. Surely, I reasoned, if it was a good issue it would bear reading and savoring again. He told me that I reminded him of a rabbi he knew who used to say things like that.

DIRECTIONS FOR REVIEWING THIS BOOK

News media will be unlikely to want to review this book. They have the power to censor ideas that they find distasteful or that might affect their profits; they just ignore them. But if they were to overcome such scruples, let me suggest the following:

There is no way to review this book in a few paragraphs. It's a book. Books develop ideas at some considerable length. They aspire to that larger vision that is wisdom (a word that seems hopelessly quaint in our media-obsessed age). Presenting a few of a book's ideas—or finding fault with them—is not the same as thinking seriously about them. So all that can be said is that you'll have to read the whole thing. It's short. The test of its value is whether the reader can ever see a newspaper the same way afterward.

Notes

Chapter 1: Why the News Can't Be Fixed
[1]Perhaps the most thoughtful (and depressing) critique is James Fallows's *Breaking the News* (New York: Pantheon, 1996).

[2]C. John Sommerville, *The News Revolution in England: Cultural Dynamics of Daily Information* (New York: Oxford University Press, 1996).

[3]CNN promotion, *Headline News Channel,* October 9, 1994.

[4]Alastair Hetherington, *News, Newspapers and Television* (London: Macmillan, 1985), p. 2.

[5]Leslie Stahl, quoted in Anna Quindlen, "Talking About the Media Circus," *New York Times Magazine,* June 26, 1994, p. 30.

[6]Michael J. Robinson and Norman J. Ornstein, "Why Press Credibility Is Going Down," *Washington Journalism Review* 12 (January 1990): 35-37.

Chapter 2: News Product as Creative Expression
[1]Mark Wiles, quoted in Ken Auletta, "Demolition Man," *New Yorker,* November 17, 1997, p. 41.

[2]Bruce McCall, "In the New Canada, Living Is a Way of Life," *New Yorker,* May 20, 1985, pp. 36-37.

[3]Local cable access broadcast, "Florida Beauty Pageant, 1988," December 14, 1988.

Chapter 3: Being Informed Versus Being Wise
[1]Barbie Zelizer, "The Image, the Word and the Holocaust" (paper presented at the Shelby Collum Davis Center Seminar, Princeton University, Princeton, N.J., March 11, 1994), pp. 1-40.

[2]E. Z. Dimitman, quoted in ibid., p. 16.

[3]Michael Medved, *Hollywood vs. America: Popular Culture and the War on Traditional Values* (New York: HarperCollins, 1992), pp. 47-48.

[4]Malcolm Muggeridge, "Reading the Signs of the Times," *Christian Herald,* June 1, 1979, p. 34.

Chapter 4: How News Schedules Drive Our Government

[1]Peggy Noonan, *What I Saw at the Revolution: A Political Life in the Reagan Era* (New York: Ballantine, 1990), pp. xvi, 103, 357.

[2]William A. Henry III, "Are the Media Too Liberal?" *Time*, October 19, 1992, p. 47.

[3]Nicholas Lemann, "Capital Crimes," *New Republic*, December 16, 1991, pp. 48-49.

[4]David Halberstam, *The Powers That Be* (New York: Dell, 1979), p. 544 (Halberstam's emphasis).

[5]Richard H. Rovere, *Senator Joe McCarthy* (New York: Harcourt, Brace & World, 1959), pp. 163-64.

[6]Daniel J. Boorstin, *The Image: A Guide to Pseudo-Events in America* (New York: Harper & Row, 1961), pp. 21-23.

[7]Halberstam, *Powers That Be*, pp. 201-14.

[8]Boorstin, *Image*, p. 16.

[9]A. J. Liebling, quoted in Gaye Tuchman, *Making News: A Study in the Construction of Reality* (New York: Free Press, 1978), p. 169.

[10]See, for example, Hedrick Smith, *The Power Game: How Washington Works* (New York: Ballantine, 1988), pp. 94-95.

[11]Anthony Smith, *Goodbye Gutenberg: The Newspaper Revolution of the 1980s* (New York: Oxford University Press, 1980), p. 44.

Chapter 5: Politics as a Perpetual Campaign

[1]Kiku Adatto, "The Incredible Shrinking Sound Bite," *New Republic*, May 28, 1990, pp. 20-23.

[2]Hedrick Smith, *The Power Game: How Washington Works* (New York: Ballantine, 1988), pp. 396-411.

[3]Daniel Bell, *The Cultural Contradictions of Capitalism* (New York: Basic Books, 1978), p. 28.

[4]Angie Cannon, "The Media Are Taking a Beating," *Gainesville Sun*, October 30, 1994, sec. E, p. 6.

Chapter 6: Why News Product Looks Nothing like History

[1]C. John Sommerville, *The News Revolution in England: Cultural Dynamics of Daily Information* (New York: Oxford University Press, 1996), pp. 64-65.

[2]Otto Friedrich, "What Really Mattered," *Time*, October 12, 1987, p. 94.

[3]Fred Barnes, "Claiming Defeat: The War and the American Press," *National Interest*, Spring 1992, pp. 100-103.

[4]Peter Paluch, "Spiking the Ukranian Famine, Again," *National Review*, April 11, 1986, pp. 33-38.

[5]Steven Emerson and Jesse Furman, "The Conspiracy That Wasn't," *New Republic*, November 19, 1991, pp. 16-31.

[6]David Halberstam, *The Powers That Be* (New York: Dell, 1979), pp. 519-20.

Chapter 7: How News Turns Science into Superstition

[1]For more on this point, see John C. Burnham, *How Superstition Won and Science Lost: Popularizing Science and Health in the United States* (New Brunswick, N.J.: Rutgers University Press, 1987), p. 239.

[2]Spencer Rich, "The Vanishing Family and Other American Myths," *Minneapolis Star and Tribune,* July 29, 1987, sec. A, p. 15.

[3]David Ignatius, "Newsmen Added to Pressure to Launch," *Gainesville Sun,* April 6, 1986. Written for the *Washington Post.*

[4]Faye Flam, "NASA PR: Hype or Public Education?" *Science,* June 4, 1993, pp. 1415-17.

Chapter 8: Polls, Statistics & Fantasy

[1]Michael Fumento, " Teenaids," *New Republic,* August 10, 1992, pp. 17-19.

[2]Daniel Benjamin, "A Mess of Misleading Indicators," *Time,* June 13, 1988, p. 49.

[3]William J. Crombie, "American Public Is Misinformed, Distrustful, New Surveys Find," *Harvard University Gazette,* December 5, 1996, pp. 1-4.

Chapter 10: Deep Theory

[1]James Fallows, *Breaking the News* (New York: Pantheon, 1996), p. 47.

[2]Conor Cruise O'Brien, "Press Freedom and the Need to Please," *Times Literary Supplement,* February 21, 1986, pp. 179-80; Benny Morris, *The Roots of Appeasement: The British Weekly Press and Nazi Germany During the 1930s* (London: Frank Cass, 1991).

Chapter 11: Virtual Society or Real Community?

[1]C. John Sommerville, *The News Revolution in England: Cultural Dynamics of Daily Information* (New York: Oxford University Press, 1996), pp. 44-45, 122-23.

[2]James Fallows, *Breaking the News* (New York: Pantheon, 1996), passim.

[3]Michael Schudson, *Discovering the News: A Social History of American Newspapers* (New York: Basic Books, 1978), pp. 93-98.

[4]Randall Rothenberg, "Politics on TV: Too Fast, Too Loose?" *New York Times,* July 15, 1990, sec. 4, pp. 1, 4.

[5]Benjamin C. Bradlee, "The Shock of the Press," *Washington Post,* July 15, 1990, sec. B, p. 1.